A YOUNG WRITER'S HANDBOOK

spilling ink

BY ANNE MAZER
AND ELLEN POTTER

ILLUSTRATED BY
MATT PHELAN

SQUARE
FISH

ROARING BROOK PRESS • NEW YORK

for
Megan Shull

SQUARE
FISH
An Imprint of Macmillan

SPILLING INK. Text copyright © 2010 by Anne Mazer and Ellen Potter.
Illustrations copyright © 2010 by Matt Phelan. All rights reserved.
Printed in the United States of America by LSC Communications,
Harrisonburg, Virginia. For information, address
Square Fish, 175 Fifth Avenue, New York, NY 10010.

Square Fish and the Square Fish logo are trademarks of Macmillan and
are used by Roaring Brook Press under license from Macmillan.

Cataloging-in-Publication Data is on file at the Library of Congress
ISBN 978-1-59643-628-2
LCCN 2010281575

Originally published in the United States by Roaring Brook Press
First Square Fish Edition: July 2012
Square Fish logo designed by Filomena Tuosto
Book design by Scott Myles
mackids.com

13   15   17   19   20   18   16   14   12

AR: 5.9 / F&P: T / LEXILE: 830L

Contents

Part III: The Writer's Brain

Appendix

Introduction

Five years ago I had two wishes: to publish a book about writing and to meet Ellen Potter. (I know, I know. In fairy tales there are always three wishes. I did have a third wish, and it came true too. But it had nothing to do with writing.)

My book was going to be called *Writer's Blocks*, and it was going to help people deal with being a writer. I had plenty of life experience: I'd worked almost thirty years as a freelance writer, had supported my family as a single parent solely on writing income, and I had grown up with writer parents. I knew the subject in my bones. But I didn't want to tell people how to write or teach them the mechanics of writing; I wanted to give them courage and an idea of what to expect. If they knew, for example, that it was normal to feel scared and stupid while writing (at least, it's normal for me!), maybe they wouldn't compare themselves so harshly to "real writers" and give up their dreams. I began to set down my thoughts on paper. I wrote pages of notes that I organized into a thick messy stack of cards with circled sentences and rubber bands and clips everywhere. And then I couldn't decide where to start the book. Every time I thought about it, I felt confused and overwhelmed. I couldn't even write a first sentence. The cards got shoved in the back of a drawer.

Meanwhile, I was getting daily letters and e-mails from kids who wanted to write. Although I didn't know Ellen Potter yet, she was getting the same letters and e-mails. The deluge of mail reminded me of another Potter (this one Harry) who had messages slipping in through the doors, the chimneys, the windows . . . There were so many kids, it seemed, who wanted to know more about writing.

As for Ellen Potter, I had wanted to meet her ever since I read an article in the local paper about her first children's book, *Olivia Kidney*. Who was this person with such a rich, layered, delicious, funny, and wicked imagination? I had to know her. But I was too shy to call her up and introduce myself. Luckily, we lived only a few miles from each other. Sooner or later, we were bound to meet.

In 2006, another children's book writer, Megan Shull, asked Ellen and me to join her on stage at the Hangar Theater in Ithaca for "You Read, Girl," an evening celebrating books, authors, and young readers. Although we had just met, there was an amazing spark between the three of us. It was an unforgettable evening and afterward, I found myself wondering how to continue the connection among Megan, Ellen, and myself.

"Maybe we can collaborate on a book about writing," I said to my new friends a few weeks later. After "You Read, Girl," wasn't "You Write, Girl," the next logical step?

Ellen, Megan, and I began to meet upstairs in the Wegman's café once a week to toss around ideas.

"It shouldn't be for girls only," was one of the first things we said. "There are lots of boys who want to write stories. This book should be for them too."

"It shouldn't be only for the kids who think they're writers."

"It should be for the kids who don't think they can write, but maybe secretly want to."

"And for those kids who haven't even considered it. Maybe they'll surprise themselves."

"It should be for as many kids as possible."

"Everyone!"

"And it has to be fun."

We were having lots of fun, huddled at a table, drinking tea, and tossing out ideas, titles, and visions. But Megan had other, more urgent projects, and Ellen and I had to go on without her. From then on, Megan would be our invisible partner, the initiator, and the one who had started everything. Without Megan, none of this would have happened.

Over to you, Ellen!

Hi, Ellen here. If you are reading this introduction right now . . . congratulations! Lots of people skip the introductions to books. The fact that you are reading this, means you are more curious than the average person. It means that you know that the secret of unearthing interesting things is to rummage around in places where other people don't bother to look. It also might mean that you are sitting in the dentist's office and have already finished the rest of our book and figured that reading our introduction was better than staring at posters about how to floss your teeth. All of this makes me think that you must be a writer deep down in your soul.

In this book, Anne and I are going to tell you some things about writing that we wish someone had told us when we were kids. We are not going to tell you that you need to follow certain rules and write outlines in order to write great stories. That would be far too easy. When you sit down to write a story, you are embarking on a wild ocean voyage. You don't know where you are going or what sort of storms you might sail into along the way. You might get shipwrecked by writer's block and have to spend a few weeks lying in the dry hot sand, looking up at the sky, telling yourself you were crazy to take this uncharted voyage in the first place. But don't worry. Another ship is sure to sail into view, and it will whisk you right back out into those tumbling, unpredictable waters of your brilliant imagination! This journey will not be easy, but it will be exciting. It will challenge every cell in your body, and just when you think you can't go on any longer, you'll find that you actually can. You, dear writer friend, are in for a great adventure. Pack this book on your journey and refer to it whenever you need a little help or some friendly words of encouragement.

Bon voyage!

Anne Mazer and Ellen Potter

Part I

Ready, Set, Go!

section

1

Is It Really This Simple?

Getting Started

by Anne

1. Pick up a pen.
2. Write a few words on paper. Like this.
3. Write whatever comes into your head—words, images, sounds, babbling, nonsense, laughter, crazy thoughts, last night's dream, a shopping list...
4. That's right—ANYTHING.

5. Keep on going. See what happens.

6. You're writing! Don't get dizzy...

Fancy Equipment Not Required

by Anne

One of the things I love about writing is that it's very low-tech. You don't need a computer (although it's nice), or have to learn a special language, or buy fancy equipment that costs a lot of money.

If you are seized by inspiration, grab the nearest thing at hand. You can scribble on the margins of a newspaper, write on the back of your science homework, use an envelope (one of my favorites), or commandeer a napkin. When I was a teen, I wrote on my jeans. (Don't do this if you wear the hundred-dollar kind.)

The physical act of writing is very easy.

The challenging part is bringing your ideas into reality.

The Blank Piece of Paper

by Anne

It's normal to feel afraid or nervous when a blank piece of paper is giving you an intimidating glare. It looks at you coldly, and says, "You think you're a writer?" Suddenly

you can't think or breathe. Your pencil slips through numb fingers and rolls under the bureau. You begin to stammer out apologies. "I didn't mean . . . I don't know . . . I can't . . ." You don't know why you wanted to write in the first place. Maybe you'll try again tomorrow. Or next week. Or in five years. The mood just isn't right.

A blank piece of paper is a formidable opponent, but you can defeat it. Just stare the thing down. Refuse to be intimidated. Take a deep breath and write a word or two on the paper. Make that a sentence, a paragraph. Now you're in charge. Now you're writing.

Writers' Rule to Ignore or Adore? Write What You Know

by Anne

When I was fifteen years old, my mother, who is a very accomplished writer, gave me a piece of writing advice. She said that I should always write what I know—about the real things that I had experienced and seen.

It was a pretty good piece of advice, but since it came from my mother, and I was a rebellious teenager, I automatically questioned it. Why should I write what I know? I fumed. Was that the limit for writers? Didn't this advice leave a lot out?

It left out imaginary worlds, for example. It left out real, but unknown, times and places. It left out putting yourself in the shoes (and mind) of a very different person than you. I ended up by concluding that there was a lot to be said for writing about what you don't know.

There's no right or wrong here. For many people, "write what you know," is an excellent guide. If you want to stick with the familiar, keep your eyes and mind open. The best writers reveal the mystery in everyday reality.

If you prefer to go as far as your imagination will take you, keep a link to reality. In Tamora Pierce's fantasy classic, *Alanna, The First Adventure*, Alanna disguises herself as a boy so that she can train as a warrior. I love the fantasy elements in this book, but what really grabs me is its truth. What girl hasn't—at least once—felt that certain worlds are only open to boys? Alanna steps into a boy's life in order to fulfill an unusual destiny. It's a thrilling idea. Even the most distant worlds have familiar problems.

What Kind of a Writer Are You?
by Anne

Do you favor exciting plots, or complex characters? Are you interested in action or emotion or mood? Do you enjoy describing everything in the room, or do you prefer to write pages of dialogue? Do you want to write about things that you've seen and experienced, or do you love fantasy worlds? Do you prefer science or fiction? Do you like romance, comedy, mystery, or stories about real-life problems? Do you like all of the above, none of it, or your own unique mixture?

Decide for yourself what kind of writer you'd like to be. Or experiment until you find what you want.

Spilling Ink

by Anne

If you're afraid to start, or you hate every word you write, here's a foolproof fear-fighting exercise. Give yourself permission to write anything. That's right—anything. Spill some ink. Just babble on paper. Or write one sentence over and over. Or close your eyes and write. (Sometimes I take off my glasses so I won't see what I'm writing.) You may be writing absolute nonsense, but you are writing. Sooner or later, you'll start to think of something you really want to write about. Or maybe, buried in the pages of sludge, there's one tiny diamond.

Official Writer's Permission Slip

_____

NOW HAS PERMISSION TO WRITE ANYTHING.

THAT MEANS SHE/HE CAN WRITE *"This is stupid"*

A THOUSAND TIMES OVER.

OR

"I am bored out of my mind and would prefer chewing on marinated shoelaces to writing this unbelievably pathetic article/story/letter/journal entry."

OR

"I wish that writing had never been invented and we all communicated with grunts and finger gestures."

OR

ANYTHING ELSE YOU WANT TO WRITE.

THIS PERMISSION SLIP HAS NO TIME LIMITS OR EXPIRATION DATE. PASS IT ON.

_____
(SIGN HERE)

section

2

Ugly First Drafts

Making a Mess

by Ellen

Before I started writing seriously, I was under the delusion that "real" writers sit down and write out the entire story in one nearly perfect, spectacularly clever draft. Oh, sure, maybe they would change a word or two, or rename one of their characters "Nathan" because his original name, "Jake," reminds them too much of their cousin Jake who belches the theme music to retro TV shows. But that's about it.

Wrong!

Hugely, profoundly, utterly wrong.

The truth of it is, professional writers have to rewrite their stories over and over (and over and over and over . . . you get the picture) again in order to get them just right. I generally spend more time rewriting than writing the first draft. My first drafts are always ugly. Super sloppy. Lots of things don't make sense. Chapters are out of sequence; some of the dialogue is confusing. The manuscript is splattered with question marks and notes to myself.

During revision the plot may change, the sequence of events may be rearranged. New characters may appear while some existing characters disappear.

keep this in mind
BY ELLEN

Have you ever read a book and thought, "This is sooo good, I could never write as well as this!" Just keep in mind that the writer may have rewritten the book twenty times before she got it right. I revised my book SLOB about a dozen times, and Anne rewrote her book The Accidental Witch thirty times over a period of seven years before she got it just right.

This is your chance to play with your work, so have fun. Mess around. See what works best. Above all, never be afraid to change things.

If you are one of those writers who dreads rewriting or thinks of it as boring, look at it this way: You know when you think of the perfect thing to say to someone five minutes after they've left the room. Don't you hate that? Well, rewriting your story gives you the chance to say the perfect thing while that person (your reader) is still "in the room." And you will look spectacularly clever in the process.

the perfect page
BY ANNE

I once met a woman who showed me a perfect page of writing. It was as good as anything I've ever read. I wanted to jump up and down and cheer as I read it. It was like reading the first page of an extraordinary novel. When I asked her if she was going to continue, she said no. She destroyed everything she wrote, she told me. Nothing measured up to her standards of perfection.

That one perfect page stands in my memory, cold and solitary, haunting me with its unfulfilled promise. She never developed her talent or shared it with the world, but what stories she might have written! If only she had had the courage to let herself make mistakes.

Whenever you feel that your writing isn't good enough, do try to make it better. But know that nothing—and no one—is perfect. Dare to write the imperfect page.

I DARE YOU Rewrite a scene from your life. Think of something that happened today. Something that wasn't perfect—maybe even something that was downright mortifying—and rewrite it as you would have wanted it to happen.

section

3

Inspiration

Showing Up On the Page

by Anne

Some writers know exactly what they want to say or write about. Others stumble on it by accident or luck. If you idly wait for inspiration, your ideas will dry up. But if you keep writing, sooner or later, inspiration will appear.

If you haven't found your ideas or inspiration yet, you have to wait. This can be frustrating, but don't quit! A lot of writing happens by deliberate accident. That means that while you work, something unexpectedly wonderful happens.

This happens to me quite often. I start work in a foul mood. I'd rather be cleaning toilets, or scrubbing floors with a toothbrush, or walking up a hill in the blazing sun, or something fun like that.

Whatever.

I sit down at my desk and start to write.

Often I'm pleasantly surprised. Instead of the unintelligible gibberish or lunatic ravings that I expect, I advance the story or even have a breakthrough.

"Eighty percent of success is showing up," Woody Allen said.

You have to show up on the page. Otherwise nothing will happen.

A Recipe for Mental Compost
by Anne

When I first discovered the idea of compost, I was so excited. No more throwing away fruit and vegetable scraps. No more waste; no more heavy garbage bags.

Instead, I dumped food scraps, rotten vegetables, and leaves onto a compost pile in the backyard. I wasn't very scientific about it, but nevertheless, months later,

I had a rich, dark, loamy soil to spread on my garden. I called it my "gardener's gold."

If you want a rich, fertile soil for your imagination, you can prepare a mental compost. The scraps are your experiences, knowledge, observations, and memories. Nothing in your life is wasted—not even your worst moments! (In fact, they make some of the richest soil.)

Here are the ingredients for "writer's gold."

Take:

• All of your embarrassing moments—the more humiliating the better. Have you ever dumped an entire tea tray with cups, saucers, milk, sugar, cookies, and of course, tea, in the lap of an important school visitor? I have. I turned this unforgettable event in my twelve-year-old life into a scene in one of my books.

• Anything you feel very, very strongly about. I've always been fascinated by people who have to hide a part of themselves to survive. My fantasy novel, *The Oxboy*, explores this subject.

• Small daily moments that capture your attention. Maybe you have a little sister who walks around with a pet mouse on her shoulders. I did! She's grown up now and still loves animals. I haven't put her in a book yet, but maybe I will some day.

• The subjects that you know a lot about. Are you a cyclist? Have you knit a sweater (it doesn't matter if the finished item came down past your knees)? Do you know how to survive in the wilderness? Do you play computer or video games? Do you know how to fold napkins into swans? All these experiences can find their way into your writing.

- What you've observed about your family and friends.

- The news, television shows, YouTube clips, advice columns . . .

- Whatever makes you laugh or cry.

- Your history: individual, family, neighborhood, town, country, world, universe . . .

- Your dreams.

- In short, your entire life.

Then:
1. Throw it all on the mental compost pile.
2. Let it sit for a while. (Time will vary from one hour to twenty-five years.)

3. It may be very helpful to take notes, or keep a journal. But it's not essential.
4. Regularly turn over the material in your mind.
5. Spread it around in your stories. Let seeds sprout from it. You'll be amazed at how many ideas it will germinate.

I DARE YOU Are you ready for excitement?
Here's how to make your own story compost pile.

1. Do nothing.
2. Repeat: Do nothing.

Yes, you heard me right. All you have to do is be aware of what is inside you.

"Aha!" you say. "I knew there was a catch!"

Maybe.

It depends how hard or easy it is for you to recognize what you carry inside you. Some people think that they are boring. Or they find life boring. Don't get caught in that trap. Pay attention to what's around you. Sift through your own life and see what gleams there. Think about what you know and what you've learned, what you've seen and observed, everything you've loved or hated. Inside this pile of experience lies your writer's gold.

Part II

Crafting Your Story

section

4

Convincing Your Characters That They Are Alive

Choosing Your Characters

by Ellen

Think about your first day at school. You're looking around the classroom, scoping out potential friends. A certain person catches your eye. Maybe it's the fact that this person has a hole in his jeans and he's doodling a map of Idaho on his kneecap. Or maybe you like the way she boldly corrects the teacher's pronunciation of her last name. This person interests you, and you'd like to get to know him or her better.

I choose my characters the way I choose my friends. They interest me. I may even admire them in certain ways. They may not be perfect—in fact, they're more interesting if they aren't—but I definitely want to know them better. So I write about them.

Hmmm, You Look Familiar: Basing Your Character on Someone You Know
by Ellen

There's nothing wrong with basing your character on someone you know, providing you make the character different enough from the real person so that no one gets offended. You can change the character's hair color; give them large, round glasses; make them a different ethnicity; or give them a different life history. Or you may want to take only two or three of the real person's outstanding qualities (i.e., her almond-shaped brown eyes, her habit of tripping over her own feet, or her sarcastic sense of humor) and apply them to your character. Do this for your own sake as well as for the real person. If your character is too much like the real person, it will be hard for you to imagine him or her riding a yak through the Himalayas, if that's what you want this character to do in your story.

The biggest advantage to basing your main character on someone you know is that you may be able to bring your character to life fairly easily. For instance, you know the way the real person tilts his head when he asks a question or the way he snorts when he laughs. It will be easier to visualize your character since you know the real-life version!

danger, danger!
BY ELLEN

When you're writing stories, never ever reveal deep, dark secrets that your friend has told you in confidence. Being a writer gives you tremendous power, so use it carefully. If you don't believe me, read Harriet the Spy, *by Louise Fitzhugh.*

I DARE YOU Think of two people you admire. Now think of the thing you admire most about each of them. Combine those two qualities into one person and write about that person in the following situation: She or he is walking down the street and a strange man hands your character a small sealed carton and says, "Don't let anything happen to this!" Then the man sprints away. What does your character do next?

Baking Characters from Scratch

by Ellen

Another way to craft your characters is to create them entirely from your imagination. This is a lot like baking cookies from scratch versus baking from a mix. When you bake your characters from scratch, you start by gathering up the different qualities that you want your main character to have.

Here's an example.

• **5 cups of cocky attitude, sifted**

• **2 cups of loyalty to friends**

• **1 cup loathing of ketchup, wet socks, and a boy from summer camp named Richard**

• **2 tablespoons of insecurity about big feet**

• **1 teaspoon of a bad habit of biting nails till they bleed**

• **One pinch of a shoe-shopping fetish (but just a pinch and no more, due to the difficulty of finding shoes for big feet)**

Combine and bake at 350 degrees or until character is done.

Creating a Main Character for Your Ingenious Story Idea

by Ellen

Do you have a mind-blowingly brilliant idea for a story but no ideas for a main character? Sometimes when you have a great story idea, it's tempting to not pay as much attention to creating great characters for the story. The truth is, though, that no matter how terrific your story idea is, you need strong characters to keep readers' interest. Without a vivid, interesting, authentic main character, even the best story idea will fall flat.

You can certainly create a character to fit your ingenious story idea; just be sure to let him or her develop fully. For example, let's say you're dying to write about an abused horse that refuses to be tamed. You're probably going to want to create a main character who is able to tame that horse, right?

idea finder

If you are fresh out of ingenious ideas—or any ideas at all—check out Section 6, "Blackberries, Raspberries, and Story Ideas," on page 33.

You'll have to ask yourself what qualities that person should have. Maybe he'll be able to sympathize with the horse because he has been treated poorly too. Or maybe he'll have an incredible gift for "talking" to animals.

Truth or Dare: Getting to Know Your Character's Deep, Dark Secrets

by Ellen

Maybe it's the sugar rush from all the junk food or the fact that you get overtired and goofy, but people tend to tell each other all their deep, dark secrets at sleepover parties.

You need to know your characters' deep, dark secrets too, in order to convince your characters that they are alive. I know that sounds weird. I know you're supposed to convince your readers that your characters are alive, not the characters themselves. But if you take the time to get to know your characters well, they will start to think and act for themselves. You'll know this is happening when ideas unexpectedly pop into your head as you write. You'll suddenly know exactly what your character would say or how they would react to something. On the other hand, if you try and make the character do something they really wouldn't do, you might feel like your story is taking a wrong turn (see "Don't Be a Bully" in Section 7 on page 55).

One way to convince your characters that they are alive is to get really nosy. Find out everything you can about them. Find out what embarrasses them, what makes them laugh, what makes them cringe. Find out how your characters react to stressful situations.

Sometimes I like to get to know my characters before I start writing. At other times, I'll plunge right into the story and find out about my characters as I'm writing. Either way, inviting your character to a sleepover party is a great way of finding out all the things they might be trying to hide from you.

Here's what you do.
• **Grab some cookies from the kitchen.**

• **Grab a notebook and a pen.**

• **Sit on your bed and pretend that your character is sitting across from you (and don't even tell me that you're too old to pretend! Writing is all about pretending).**

• **Eat a cookie.**

ar character the following questions; then
down their answers. They will answer you, I
ise. At first it will feel like the answers are coming from your own brain, but you are sort of sharing
a brain with your character at this point. You are
imagining what it is like to be them (a very useful
skill, both in writing and in life!).

Here are the questions (feel free to make up your own too).

1. What is your happiest memory?
2. What makes you laugh so hard soda shoots out of your nose?
3. What don't you want anyone to find out about you?
4. What is the best part of your personality?
5. What shoes do you usually wear?
6. Name some things that you are not very good at.
7. How would your best friend describe how you look?
8. What irritates you (i.e., noises, bad habits, personality traits)?
9. What are you afraid of?
10. Tell me about your family.
11. What does your bedroom look like?
12. What do you think of yourself when you look in the mirror?
13. What's the most embarrassing thing that has ever happened to you?
14. Do you have a crush on anyone?

Now pay attention. Here is the number one most important question you can ask your character. Ready?

15. What do you really, REALLY want more than anything else in the world.

Heart's Desire
by Ellen

Discovering what your character wants—I mean really, really wants—is the single most important thing you can find out about your character. It might be an object, like an electric guitar. It might be that your character wants a friend. It might be that your character wants to feel good about himself. Your character's heart's desire is what propels your story forward. If your story were a car, your character's heart's desire would be the engine.

Think about what you're doing right this second. You're reading *Spilling Ink*. Why? Maybe it's because you want to kill some time before you go to soccer practice. Maybe it's because your aunt gave you this book for your birthday and you're going to see her this Saturday and you know that she's going to ask you how you liked it. Or maybe it's because you really, really want to be an author. Whatever the reason, you are reading this book because you want something. In fact, if you think about nearly everything that you do in a day, you can trace it back to a "want." The same goes for your character. As you write your story, always try to think about what your character wants, from the tiniest want to the heart's desire.

I DARE YOU

Make a list of all the things you want. It can be anything from wanting a particular bully to leave you alone, to wanting riding lessons, to wanting your best friend to move back from Japan. Now pick the thing on the list you want the most and think of all the ways you could attain that thing, from the realistic to the ridiculous. Write a short scene in which you try out one of those ideas, and see what happens.

Naming Your Characters

The Name Game

by Ellen

I love the process of naming my characters. Finding the right name for your character is often the first step in convincing your characters that they are alive. Not only is it a great way to get to know them, but it's also just plain fun. I go about finding names in several different ways.

1. Read the phone book. You'll be amazed at some of the strange names you find. (I found the names Strawberry Lemon and Axel Greasy in one of my phone books. I wrote them down in my journal and am still waiting for the chance to use them in a book.)

2. Baby-name books are a great resource, with the added bonus that you learn what each name means. Knowing the origin and meaning of your character's name can deepen your understanding of the character. Even if you're writing fantasy, you can find some otherworldly sounding names that might work beautifully.

3. You can make up the name out of your imagination. Sit quietly with a pen and paper and think about your character's personality. Start jotting down any names that pop into your head. Just mess around with different sounds. Pair a long first name with a short last name or vice versa. When you're done, read over your list of names and consider the first impressions that those names give you.

4. If you keep a journal (and I strongly suggest that you do), write down names that catch your attention. Some day, one of those names might be the

perfect match for a character. (That's exactly what happened with my character Olivia Kidney. See Section 19, "Journaling" and "The Story of You," on page 174.)

section

6

Blackberries, Raspberries, and Story Ideas

The Berry Patch

by Anne

Years ago, I lived in a tiny apartment surrounded by acres of fields. Blackberries, blueberries, and raspberries grew wild there. On summer days, I went out with a pail. Thorns scratched my arms and tore my clothes. I came home with stained fingers and no appetite. What I loved most of all was the overflowing, crazy generosity of nature.

When I think about ideas, I think of the berry patch. Did you know that ideas are everywhere, growing wild, yours for the picking? If you miss one or two, nature will offer you many more. Don't ever worry about running out of ideas. They're infinite. They're all around you.

And everyone has them—even if they don't realize it.

Where Do You Get Your Ideas?

by Anne

If there were a top ten list of questions for writers, "Where do you get your ideas?" would be number one.

A very famous writer once answered the question by saying something like, "the third aisle of Woolworth's, on the bottom shelf."*

Good answer! Even unusual ideas come from ordinary places.

Mine come from my life and experiences, my wishes and dreams, hopes and disappointments. I also get ideas from family and friends, from total strangers, from people I glimpse on a bus, things I've overheard by accident, and from what I read in books or newspapers.

Whether you get your ideas from an overheard conversation in the supermarket line, from a family story, from a

*That was Stephen King. And it might be the second shelf in the fourth aisle, I don't remember. Woolworth's (what we used to have instead of Kmart and Target) has gone out of business since Mr. King wrote that article. I don't know where he gets his ideas now.

dream, from the worst/best thing that happened when you were seven, or from a lifetime of reading adventure stories, it's easy to point to "where it came from." It's harder and much more interesting to explain how an idea comes together.

For me, at least, ideas are rarely born fully formed. They take a long time to develop. Many of my ideas sit in my files for seven years, or longer, before I know what to do with them. For example, my fantasy novel, *The Oxboy*, began with a poem that I wrote one evening with a good friend. The two of us were both writers and mothers of small children, and neither of us had enough writing time. So we decided to meet once a week to write together. Using a line of poetry, or a random sentence as a jumping off point, we wrote as fast as we could. It was wild, exhilarating fun— for a writer. I didn't expect anything serious to come out of these sessions, but in one of them I wrote the poem that inspired *The Oxboy*. I don't remember how the poem began, but I do remember the deep and powerful feeling I had as I wrote it. "The ox was far kinder than the man had been." This line showed up out of nowhere and wouldn't leave me alone. It echoed in my head for months. The idea of an animal being more human than a human being fascinated me. Yet it wasn't enough to work with. I tried over and over to write a story about it and failed every time. Luckily I had a second, unrelated idea rolling around in my mind. It was about a boy who kept a talking animal under his bed at night. One day the two ideas merged in my mind. I began to write a book about a boy who was half human, half animal, and who lived in a world where he had to hide his animal nature in order to survive. When I look back, I can never figure out how it all happened in the first place. "How did I think of putting those things together?" I ask myself. "And how did they lead to the world of the oxboy?"

There's a mystery about the creative process. It can never be completely defined or understood. Are good ideas fated? Do they come by accident? Or do they need a writer who's stubborn enough to keep on trying until she finds what works?

You Dare Me!
by Anne

"Okay," I can hear you say, "maybe you have ideas, but I don't." You fold your arms across your chest and scowl at me. "I dare you to find a single idea in my head," you say.

Yes, I'll take that dare . . . Here's what I might find in your head right now:

- Desire to play with the kitten your family found wandering by the side of the road and rescued.

- Seething anger at the gym teacher who forced you to turn a somersault in front of the entire class. Everyone saw the rip in the bottom of your pants.

- Total boredom at having to sit through yet another school awards assembly, especially since you have never received a single one.

- Plots of revenge against your older sister who read your diary and laughed at it.

- Happiness that you won a major part in the school play; but fear that you'll forget your lines.

- Dreams of another world that can only be seen in the reflection of your glasses . . .

Any one of these could be the germ of a story. (This is one kind of germ you want to catch!) But I'm not a mind reader. There might be something even more intriguing happening in your head right now. Take a look and see.

Make an Idea Catcher

by Anne

You might think you don't have ideas. But you almost certainly do. There are two possibilities:

You don't know where to look for your ideas.

You already have lots of ideas. You just don't realize it yet.

You can train your "idea-catching" brain. When an idea whizzes past you, be ready to grab it.

Here's how to do it.

1. Turn on your idea antenna. Remind yourself every morning that you're going to keep a corner of your brain alert for ideas. Then check in a couple of times a day. "Any ideas, Brain?" you might ask. Or, "Did you see or hear or experience anything you want to remember?" If the answer is yes . . .

2. Have a place to note your ideas, such as a notebook, computer, electronic device, or sketch pad.

3. Have regular "idea-collecting times." First thing in the morning and last thing at night are both excellent. A dream might give you an idea, or you might remember something that happened during the day.

4. If an idea hits unexpectedly, grab the nearest piece of paper, or even the back of your hand, to write it down.

5. Please don't get nervous if at first you don't seem to have good ideas. It takes time to be able to recognize them. And sometimes you get a stream of ideas that go nowhere. I often remind myself that one good idea is sometimes enough to keep me busy for years. But that really powerful idea might take it's time to show up.. So relax and be patient with yourself.

   If you're like me and get tense when people tell you to stay relaxed, it's okay. Ideas will still get through. Think of them as termites boring through the floor. They'll find a way in.

6. Don't be afraid of your own thoughts. Lots of people prejudge their ideas as "crazy" or "stupid." Are you sure they are? Let's check out a few of my published ideas: a boy who's half-human, half-animal, and who keeps a talking animal under his bed? Two sisters, one of whom has magic and the other doesn't? A boy who transforms his room into a forest to make a home for a salamander? A girl who loves to write and who feels she's not as special as the rest of the people in her family? Do any of these ideas shout "best-seller" or "award-winning" or even "published work" to you? I won't be offended if you say no. In the cold light of reality, ideas don't always look like much. Contrary to what people

think, the idea doesn't make the story; it's what you bring to the idea. It's your imagination, enthusiasm, and vision that turn a silly, stupid, or strange idea into storytelling gold.

Be sure to write down all your ideas. Let them flow onto paper. Maybe they're not so bad. Maybe they're actually kind of intriguing. If they spark your imagination, they're definitely good. Who knows where they'll lead you? Once you have them written down, let your ideas sit. Later, you can decide if you want to keep them or not.

7. Be playful with your ideas. Write them on scraps of paper, put them in a bowl, and randomly pick two or three. Then try to write a story from them.

8. If you can't get any ideas at all, you can build on other people's ideas. You can take a line from someone else's story and write your own story from it. You can find ideas in movies, television shows, songs, comic books, the news, or in a family story. You can also take a favorite character and write a story about him or her. This is different from copying someone else's words. We all can and should be inspired by other people's work.

9. Have brainstorming sessions with a friend.

The more you look for ideas, the more you'll see them. Soon they'll be swarming around you!

Advanced Idea Catchers (P.S. They aren't hard.)

by Anne

1. Notice what thoughts jump into your brain when you quit writing. Have a notepad or scrap paper ready to write them down.

2. Turn on a secret tape recorder or movie camera in your brain. Okay, don't put your ear to your brother's door and try to hear his private conversations. But do keep your ears open for curious sentences

that might fly by. Like, "Mom, can I take a salamander home?" (Yes, I did overhear that one.) Listen to your friends' and classmates' conversations. Listen to how they speak and what they say.

3. Go to the mall. Although I dislike malls, there's always a lot of interesting stuff going on. The mall is like a museum of stuff. You can people watch in the food court. You can stare at the odd gadgets in the electronic stores, such as a fortune-telling telephone or a radio in the shape of a tooth. (Guess which one is real and which I made up.) You can note the many types of hair ribbons and/or compare comic book heroes.

When I had to take one of my kids on a shopping trip to the mall, I often found inspiration for the Abby Hayes series there—even if I wasn't looking for it. For example, I'd always be amazed at the calendar kiosks that sprung up before the holidays and would stop to look at them, even if I was in a rush. There were calendars about outhouses, movie stars, barns, mountain ranges, duct tape, sunsets, puzzles, race cars, words, pigs, mushrooms, rivers, cows, knitting, clouds, state parks, and every type of dog in existence. Since each chapter in an Abby book begins with a quote from a fictitious calendar, the mall calendars inspired me into wild fits of imagination. I had great fun inventing calendars for Abby with names like the "Marshmallow" calendar or the "Daily Eyeglass" calendar or the "Supermarkets of New Jersey" calendar.

You don't have to go to the mall for accidental inspiration, of course. Some writers find themselves flooded with ideas in museums, libraries, summer camp, apartment buildings, parks, or schools. Or even in their own homes.

4. Keep a dream diary. Writers can unlock characters, story ideas, images, feelings, and experiences through their dreams. Some writers use dreams as jumping-off points for stories or poems. I started keeping a dream diary in high school and have continued for most of my life.

After doing any of these five exercises, do you notice any difference? Are you more aware of your thoughts or the things that are happening around you?

How to Turn Off Your Brain and Turn On Your Ideas

by Anne

You don't always have to work hard to find ideas. Sometimes you need to relax to let your creative mind do its best work. Wasting time, doing nothing, and even sleeping can be some of your most important writer's tools. Be sure to cultivate them. They are an endless source of fresh creativity.

Sometimes ideas only show up when they think you're not watching. They're like mice that wait until the family has gone to bed before they creep out of the floorboards. But even if you're half asleep, you can still keep a tiny part of your mind alert for when an idea tiptoes out.

It's like turning on a twenty-four-hour movie camera. You forget it's there but, nevertheless, it keeps recording. You may be deeply involved in a chess game or a swimming tournament, or making a necklace, or gossiping with friends, but at the same time, in a very quiet corner of your mind, a writer is watching. Or perhaps you really are doing nothing. Let your mind roam where it will, but remain gently watchful.

I get ideas while waiting in lines, staring at the clouds, or lying sick in bed. Ideas show up when I'm washing dishes, waiting for an appointment, or, especially, out on a walk. (The idea to do this book came on a walk. I worked out a lot of its sections while hiking in the woods.) And I've learned from experience to always keep a pen and pad next to my computer, because as soon as I decide that I'm done writing for the day, ideas show up in hordes.

---

brainstorming
BY ANNE

Brainstorming describes the perfect storm of mental activity, accompanied by lightning flashes and loud rumbles of thunder, which occurs when you're thinking up ideas at a rapid pace. I like to imagine dark, towering purple clouds being blown across my mind by a high wind, or perhaps on the march like an army. Ideas have a way of swooping down and conquering your mind; the term brainstorm *captures this beautifully. Flashes of insight illuminate the mental landscape. You see with startling clarity. Old, tired ways of thinking are swept away. Nothing is better than a good creative storm!*

section

7

Now We Get to the Weird Stuff: Plot

To Plot or Not to Plot
by Ellen

I'm about to tell you something that might shock you.

Here it is: I never plot out my books.

I don't write story outlines; I don't think about themes before I start writing. Frankly, I often don't know what's going to happen from one page to the next. I just stalk my characters. I become a sort of "character groupie," following close enough behind them to see what they will do. They nearly always do something far more interesting than anything I might have thought up if I had outlined the plot beforehand.

I usually have a vague idea of what the story will be about because I generally know beforehand what my main character really, really wants (see "Heart's Desire" in Section 4 on page 28). Sometimes I have an inkling of what might happen in the near future, or there may be a cool scene that I would love to include toward the end of the book. Still, I try not to get too attached to any ideas in advance, in case the story wants to go in a different direction.

Although it's often scary to write this way, I like not knowing what's going to happen next. If I knew what was going to happen next, I'd probably be too bored to write the story. When I write without an outline, I am constantly surprised by my story, and if I'm surprised then my readers probably will be too.

Now, if you read the introduction to this book (no hard feelings if you haven't; read it when you can't think of anything else to do), you know that Anne and I are only giving you suggestions about writing. There are virtually no rules in this book. We're only telling you what works best for us. If writing without knowing your plot ahead of time makes you want to stick your tongue in an electric socket, then please, by all means, write an outline for your story! Many writers outline their books before they start. Or you might want to write an outline for a few pages at a time so that you are still leaving room for the story to go in unexpected directions. In other words, the technique that works best for you is the best technique to use.

Stalking the Wild Character
by Ellen

If you want to try writing a story without a plot outline, but doing so seems as crazy as traveling across Outer Mongolia without a map, don't worry. You do have a map. Your map is your character's desires. If you follow your character from desire to desire, you will be creating your plot along the way.

Here's what I mean.

Let's say your main character, whose name is Lindsay, really, really wants to get the lead in the school play. That is her heart's desire. Okay, now you know that the story is probably going to center around the school play, the auditions, and the other people who also want the lead.

Once you know Lindsay's heart's desire, your job is to make it hugely difficult for her to get it. I mean, if

Lindsay wants the lead in the play and poof, she gets the lead in the play, there's no story, is there? Making it hard for Lindsay to get her heart's desire raises the stakes in your story. Your readers are going to start rooting for her. They're going to want to see her succeed, and they'll be biting their nails every time it looks like she might not.

Okay, let's make things difficult for Lindsay: Maybe she lives in a tiny apartment with five siblings, and there's never any quiet space to practice her monologue for the audition. What if her parents feel that acting is a waste of time? What if she has to work after school in her family's grocery store, which means she wouldn't be able to attend the audition?

Lindsay's minor wants are important too. They'll help guide you through your story's subplots. Subplots are simply side stories that generally tie into the main story. They give the story layers and help move the action forward. For example, let's say there is an eccentric elderly woman named Mrs. Phupette who shops at Lindsay's family's store. Lindsay is fond of her, and when Mrs. Phupette falls ill with pneumonia and needs her groceries delivered, Lindsay asks to be the one to deliver them to her . . . there's a subplot created by a smaller want. Mrs. Phupette, it turns out, had once been a stage actress, and when she finds out about Lindsay's heart's desire, she offers to coach her. While unpacking the groceries, Lindsay recites her audition piece, occasionally using bagels and turnips as props, and Mrs. Phupette gives her valuable acting tips.

Of course, the subplot doesn't have to involve Lindsay directly. You can have a subplot centered around another character. What if, for example, Lindsay's dad is worried that the new Shop-Till-You-Plotz Supermarket opening around the corner will put his little grocery out of business? And what if the stuck-up daughter of Shop-Till-You-Plotz's owner is none other than Lindsay's competition for the lead in the school play? Once again you'll need to follow that other character's desires and make sure that the subplot is important to the whole story. You can tell if you have a good subplot by this simple test: Try cutting the subplot out of your story. If the story doesn't work without it—or seems flat and less interesting—you have a good subplot.

Now that you have your map (it's a rough map, but it's a beginning), you are ready to stalk your character. Before I start writing, I get really quiet. I close my eyes. I imagine a setting. I try to see it as vividly as possible—all its sounds and colors and smells. This is the first place in which I'm going to plunk down my main character. This is also the place where I am going to start my journey as a groupie/stalker, and I need to get my bearings. Once I can see the setting clearly, as well as any other characters that might be in the vicinity, I look at my main character. I think about my character's heart's desire. I think about his or her challenges. I think about everything I might already know about my character. I also think about my minor characters. What do they want and how do their desires affect the main's character's desires? Then I boot up my laptop and wait for my character to do something or say something.

She or he will, I promise.

It might be something that makes no sense to you. It doesn't matter. Write it down and keep watching and listening. If you get stuck, ask your character what he or she wants at this moment. It doesn't have to be the heart's desire. It might be as trivial as "she wants to read the note that her friend has passed to her during class." Have her read the note (or not—the note might get confiscated by the teacher), then see what happens next. Let the story unfold on its own. (Remember, it's entirely possible for your character to have a change of heart as the story progresses, which means that his or her heart's desire may change too.) Anytime you get stuck, once again, ask the character what she wants now. You can also ask this of other characters in the scene, of course, and then the map becomes even more interesting. Always keep your main character's heart's desire in the back of your mind, like an ultimate destination, but be prepared to travel through lots of dark alleys and interesting side roads to get there.

You Can Ignore What I Just Said

by Ellen

You don't actually have to know your character's heart's desire before you start writing. You can gradually figure out what your character wants as you are writing and getting to know your character better. It's slightly scarier to write this way, and you may have to cut out some false starts when you revise, but give it a try.

I DARE YOU What were your subplot(s) today? I guarantee you had at least one subplot. Think about the little things that happened to you today (i.e., you lost your math book and had to find it before school, you had a bit of lunchroom pizza stuck to the front of your shirt and a certain someone saw it before you could flick it off, etc.). Write about that subplot, and see how it tied into other, more major events.

Oops, What Happened?
What to Do When Your Story Is
Going in the Wrong Direction

by Ellen

It never fails. I'll be happily typing away, confident that my story is coming along just great, when all of a sudden . . . uh-oh! I realize that I've somehow taken a wrong turn. Maybe the main character's "exciting" summer trip to Spain has turned into a big snooze. Or maybe the story is beginning to center much more around the main character's little sister than the main character herself. Any time your story starts to go off course, it's unnerving. In fact, getting lost in your story is a lot like getting lost in real life. You panic. I always do, anyway. At first. Then I try to calm down, look around. Am I really lost? Or have I simply discovered another, far more interesting route?

Follow Your Passion

by Ellen

Sometimes you need to write pages and pages of the story you thought you were writing to discover the story that you are actually writing.

Let's say you start out writing a story about a girl who finds a secret room in her family's new house that

transports her to ancient Egypt. But as the story progresses, you find that you are devoting too many pages
to a subplot about the girl's younger brother who has
cerebral palsy and is trying to fit in at a new school. Suddenly, the ancient Egypt adventure is getting smothered
by the little brother's story.

Instead of forcing your story to go the way you first
imagined it would, keep an open mind. If you are moving
away from your original story idea, it might be because you
don't really feel that passionate about it. Nothing wrong
with that. In fact, everything is right with that, since you
need to feel passionate about your story in order to tell it
well! You may want to turn your main plot into a subplot,
or even delete it altogether. Never be afraid to change your
story midway. All writers do that at some time or another.
Be sure to keep copies of all your drafts, though, in case
you decide to stick with the original story after all.

Here Is Something You Can Do with Deleted Sections of Your Story

by Ellen

Print them out, stick them in an envelope, and mail them
to your best friend. Tell her or him to hold the letter for
you without opening it, and then give it back to you in

three months. When you open it and read it fresh, you
might be inspired to write a new story with it.

P.S. My theory is that three months is a magic time
period. It takes three months to . . . break (or develop)
a habit, really get to know someone, or grow out a
bad haircut.

Don't Be a Bully!
by Ellen

You don't like to be told what to do, and neither do your
characters. Once you've convinced your characters that

they are alive, they are going to have wills of their own. You may want them to do certain things in the story, but if it isn't in their nature to do those things, they're going to rebel. They do this by making sure your story falls flat on its face.

When you feel like you've lost your way in your story, don't automatically trash your initial storyline. It may be absolutely fine. Instead, you might want to take a look at your "sleepover party" notes to reconnect with your characters' basic personalities. For instance, have you made your character more trusting than he really is, just to make your story idea work? Would your character really be fooled by the clearly menacing man wearing the red scarf who is lurking outside his home? Would your character really walk off with him?

"But you don't understand! My character has to walk off with the man in the red scarf, or my story won't work!" you protest.

Instead of bullying your character to do what you want him to do, experiment by letting your character do what you think he really would do in that situation. If you think he would make a run for it, let him. See where the ensuing chase will lead you. It might take the story in a direction you hadn't imagined.

The Plot Thickens:
Confessions of a Series Writer

by Anne

Different techniques can work for different writers.
They can even work for the same writer. I write series
books in a very different way than I write stand-alone
novels. For a stand-alone novel, I don't worry about
plotting. Like Ellen, I allow myself a lot of uncertainty.
I wander around, explore, get lost, and follow whims.
But when I write a series book, I need a clearer map of
what lies ahead.

When I begin an Abby Hayes book, for example,
I know my characters, and I know what sort of painful
situation they're soon going to find themselves in. For
example, here's what I started with for one book: Abby
invites a new friend on a camping trip and hopes that her
family won't embarrass her.

I usually know where the story is going to end
up too. Of course, Abby's family embarrasses her, but
she and her new acquaintance, Hannah, become great
friends anyway.

However, I don't know—and I don't want to know—
everything that will happen from start to finish. That
would take all the fun out of writing! I'd have to hang up
my pen and find a more exciting job, like sweeping up

carrot peelings. So I never plot my books in advance, or print out an outline, or map my book on a giant piece of paper. Instead I begin with a rough idea in my head. I know I'm starting at point A and that I'll end up at point Z, and I might have a few sketchy ideas of what could possibly happen in between. But usually I work those out as I write the book.

My family went on lots of camping trips when I was growing up, so I was easily able to imagine all the things that might go wrong for Abby. What if the tents are close together, and Abby and Hannah can hear loud snoring from one of them? What if her sisters fight the whole time? What if her brother whines? What if her parents are always on their cell phones? What if they go to pick blueberries and get sick from eating too many? Or if they go on a hike and get lost in the woods?

These are the kinds of questions I asked myself as I wrote the book *Too Close For Comfort*, one of my favorite Abby books. But they were only a guide. There was still plenty of room for surprise and spontaneity. Things happened that I never anticipated. For example, Brianna showed up on a yacht and tried to make Hannah her friend. What did Abby do then? The plot didn't really thicken; it twisted and turned and carried the story along with it.

Plot Till You Drop:
What I Learned from Writing a Series

by Anne

Before series, I was an obsessed, perfectionist writer who took two or more years to write a novel, and who often experienced short but painful bouts of writer's block. A big part of my writer's block was that I didn't know how to plot. The process of figuring out what happened next in a story intimidated me. Okay, it terrified me. How did writers "make" their story work? It was a total mystery to me.

Not too surprisingly, the first book I wrote received six almost identical rejection letters that said, "Lovely writing, but no plot." Even though I somehow managed to publish three novels after that, the word *plot* still sent shivers of fear up my spine.

Then along came Abby. I hadn't been looking to write a series, but when an editor from Scholastic called and asked if I was interested, I said, "Sure." Because, well ... why not? The editor asked me to write a sample three chapters. I sat down at my computer and dashed off the sample in an afternoon. I didn't worry about the plot because I didn't particularly care if I got the job or not. I thought, I'm not going to do this if it isn't easy. Famous last words! I had no idea how hard I was going to work for the next decade of my life.

A few weeks later, I got a call. They wanted me to write the series. Thinking about it more seriously, I decided that I couldn't turn down a steady gig. I was a single parent with two children, and I needed to make a living. Besides, I really loved the idea we had come up with: a series about a girl who loved to write and who also kept trying to improve herself. That seemed tailor made for me.

Scholastic signed me up to write six books, each approximately eighty to one hundred pages long. Because they wanted to publish the books quickly, I had seven weeks to write the first one. I worked out an initial plot idea with my first editor and sat down at my computer. There is only one word to describe my mental state: *panic!* Complete, utter, total panic.

In spite of my panic, I made a very important decision. Even if I only had seven weeks and was under a lot of pressure, I wasn't going to dash off the book. I would use all of my skills and abilities to write the best book I possibly could. I would revise when the story needed revising and take time to polish every chapter. To my surprise, I still made the deadline.

Today, after writing twenty-two Abby Hayes books and six Sister Magic books, I'm a different writer. I'm no longer afraid of plotting; in fact, I feel very comfortable with it. Series writing transformed some of my habits and many of the ways I thought about writing. Hey, I'm still obsessed and a perfectionist, but writer's block doesn't stop me the way it used to. And I learned that I was capable of a lot more than I realized.

Snap, Crackle, and Plot: Thinking Up Plot Ideas
by Anne

Once you know the character—her family, friends, and world—it's a snap. Have you ever played with action figures, stuffed animals, or dolls? Have you sent them on adventures or made up stories for them? Figuring out new Abby Hayes ideas was exactly like that.

My wonderful Abby Hayes editor, Kate, and I would get together on the phone to discuss the next Abby. Our conversations would go something like this:

Kate: So, Anne, what would you like to do for the next book?

Anne: Um, I don't know. (Thinks a minute.) What if Abby tries out for a part in the school play? And if she doesn't get the part she hopes for?

Kate: I love that idea! And what if one of her best friends, like Natalie, gets it instead?

Anne: Ooooh. That's great! Natalie will turn out to be an acting genius. Abby will be only so-so. And she'll be really discouraged.

Kate: But then I see her finding a way to use her true talents.

Anne: Yeah! What if she rewrites the play?

Making up plots was this easy—and this much fun. Of course, then I'd actually have to do the writing . . . and that wasn't easy at all.

As I Was Saying . . . Um, What Exactly Was I Saying?

by Anne

The hardest part of writing a series isn't plotting or characters or coming up with new ideas. It's remembering what I've already written. There are twenty-two books in the Abby Hayes series. Sometimes I can't even remember all the titles, much less the twists and turns of the plots, names of minor characters, descriptions of major characters (e.g., the color of Abby's eyes), and so on. I have been known to check Wikipedia to remind myself of important details in my series. Please don't tell anyone.

The Strange and Wonderful World of Series

by Anne

Writing a series isn't the same as writing a plain old novel. Here are some of the differences:

1. You're on a very tight schedule. Although I had less than two months for the first Abby Hayes, immediately after that my schedule relaxed (sort of) and I had three, and then four months to do each book. It was a point of honor for me to meet every single deadline for every single book. My insanely responsible behavior inspired the serious, conscientious Mabel in the Sister Magic series.

2. You work more collaboratively. I loved this part of series writing. I loved tossing ideas back and forth with Kate. It's how I learned to plot. It was so much fun. It was very supportive. It wasn't as lonely as writing can sometimes feel.

3. When you write a series, you have to respect the characters and the world that you've created. You can't go off into crazy directions, as creative or fascinating as they might be. Abby Hayes is an ordinary girl who loves to write. I can't have her suddenly time travel to ancient Rome, become a singing superstar, work in a factory for pennies a

day, or be the pampered only child of rich newspaper moguls.

4. Your character lives in "series time." Abby Hayes spent three years in fifth grade. Many alert readers wrote me to complain: "Why does she have summer vacation and then start fifth grade all over again?" Good question that I don't know how to answer, alert readers! I was so very relieved when Abby finally moved up to sixth grade. I was also at the point where if I had to write one more scene set in a fifth-grade classroom, my brain was going to explode. (And you know how messy it is to clean brains off computer keyboards.)

5. You have to figure out how to keep the plots fresh and engaging. Even after ten, fifteen, or twenty books! Fortunately, I enjoy that kind of challenge. Here's what I learned.

Introduce something new in each book. It can be a new setting, such as a trip or a move; or a totally new character; or something surprising about an old character, like when law-abiding Abby broke the rules and got in trouble.

Have a good time. The Hayes family trip to Paris was so much fun for me to write. First of all, I used to live in Paris when I was a student, so it brought back lots of good memories. And then I got to spoof airline travel and some of the embarrassing, awkward, or silly parts of being a tourist.

Believe in your idea. I wrote two Abby books about crushes. In both, Abby feels confused, uncertain, and uncomfortable. I don't think I could have written a flirty, romantic-type novel—although some of my readers definitely wanted me to. I wrote the stories in a way that made sense to me.

Have a strong emotional connection to the story. In one book, Abby's family moves to a bigger, fancier house that is far away from their old neighborhood. Abby struggles to adjust to this move, which isolates her from her friends. When I wrote this story, I felt all the pain (and comedy) of moving. I had a lot of experience to draw on: I've moved many, many times in my life, although I lost track after the thirtieth move. A lot of kids have written me to say that story is one of their favorite Abby books.

Who Is Telling Your Story? The Narrative Voice

Finding the Right Narrative Voice

by Ellen

I'm sure you can think of a time when two people told you about the same incident and their stories were totally different. It's not necessarily that one or the other was lying. They just each had their own point of view.

When you start a story, you should think about the narrative voice, which is just a fancy term for the person who's telling the story. There are several types of narrative voices. Here they are (don't get put off by the complicated terms. It's pretty simple stuff).

Me, Myself, and I: First-Person Narrative

by Ellen

This is when one of the characters in the story is narrating. It can be a main character or one of the minor characters. You can generally recognize first-person narrative right away because the narrator uses the pronoun *I*. For instance:

I blew out the candles and made a wish. That was when my world turned wonky.

For me, first-person is the coziest narrative voice. Reading a story that is written in the first person reminds me of sitting on the front porch, sipping a tall glass of lemonade, and listening to someone tell me a tale about something that happened to him. The person telling the story is a stranger to me. However, as he talks, I get to know more and more about him. Also I start to care more about him, which makes me care more about his story.

Before I start telling a story in first-person narrative, I often take a long walk. To a casual observer, I just look like someone who is fascinated by the crows cruising the cornfields or the goofy chocolate lab bouncing around in someone's yard. But really, I'm listening to a voice in my head . . . the voice of my narrator.

Now, if you've done some of the character development beforehand, this voice may not be as hard to hear as you might think. You may already know your narrator pretty well, and hearing her voice will come naturally. As I said before, though, I don't always develop my characters before I start writing. Some of them begin to form during the act of writing. If this is the case for your narrator, you may just have to listen longer before you hear a voice come through.

Try imagining sitting on the front porch with your narrator, sipping that icy lemonade. "So . . .," you say to her, "tell me what happened. Tell me all about it." Then listen. The voice may be fuzzy at first. It may sound suspiciously like your own voice chattering in your head. Never mind. Just keep listening until the voice becomes clearer and more itself. Listen for the voice's rhythm: Is it slow and calm? Hyper? Listen for the general tone of the voice. Is it sarcastic or bubbly or wisecracking? Are there expressions that keep getting repeated? An accent?

When I start to walk faster in order to get home and start writing, I know that I've begun to "nail" my narrative voice.

Now, although this method works for me, it may not work for you. It may seem too wacky. That's fine. Ignore it. Throughout this book you'll keep hearing us say that there are no rules in writing (even the grammatical rules can be broken, as long as you do it for a reason and not just because you don't know the rule). As with so many things, you'll have to figure out what works best for you.

Here are a few more suggestions for developing a strong first-person narrative:

- Write a diary entry in your narrator's voice (e.g., about walking in the woods and finding a dead body).

- If you are loosely basing your narrator on someone you know, pay lots of attention to that person when he or she is talking. Notice any unusual phrases that the person uses.

- Tape-record yourself talking in what you imagine is your narrator's voice.

- Think of three different characters and have each of them narrate the same scene.

It's All About You: Second-Person Narrative
by Ellen

This is when the narrator talks about "you" as the subject. For instance:

You walked to the bakery and bought a doughnut. After you had devoured it in the store, you told the man behind the counter that it was stale and you wanted another one.

The second-person narrative voice isn't used very much. It might be interesting to try it, though. It could work in a story in which someone is telling a story directly to someone else, and that story is about the person listening (such as when parents tell their children about something they did as a baby). Or it can have an angry, accusatory sound to it, as in:

I asked you to the school dance, and you told me you were going to Venezuela for your grandmother's funeral, but here you are slow dancing with Walter McVeety!

Third-Person Narrative Put Yourself in Their Shoes: Third-Person Limited

by Ellen

Here, the story is told from the point of view of a character, but someone else is telling the story. Let's put ourselves back on that porch, sipping lemonade. This time, the stranger is telling us a story about someone he knows really, really well.

This is a great narrative voice to use when you want to get inside the head of one main character. We are seeing the story through this character's eyes, feeling what he or she feels, thinking what he or she thinks. Third-person limited is a powerful way to get your readers to identify with your main character without using the character's voice to tell the story, as in a first-person narrative. Here's an example.

Robert smelled the creature's rotted breath as he struggled to free himself. The rough ropes cut into his skin painfully, but he resisted the urge to cry out for help.

The third-person limited can have a distinct personality. Remember, the stranger on the porch may not be telling the story about himself, but he is still telling the story in his voice. You can give the narrative voice personality in several different ways. For instance, if you use short sentences without a lot of description, you give the story a very plain, direct sound. Fast. No fuss, no muss. Maybe a little hard-edged. If you are writing an action-packed story, this sort of tone might work really well. Here's an example.

Brenda was desperate. Frantic. Her right foot slipped off the edge of the windowsill. She screamed. The

people below screamed. Suddenly a hand reached out of
the window. It grabbed her ponytail.

Using longer sentences with loads of description
gives a totally different personality to the narrative voice.
The sound is richer; the narrative is more observant.
The pace may be slower too. The stranger on the porch
wants you to settle back and imagine the story at a lei-
surely pace. Lots of fantasy stories take on this tone, for
instance:

Deep in the forest, surrounded by a grove of ancient
hemlock trees, was a stone cottage covered with moss. Its
roof was old and battered, and its green shutters hung off
the windows at odd angles. It was strangely silent there.
The birds didn't sing, and the wind didn't fuss with the
tree branches. The only sound came from inside a rusty
tin washtub that stood by the front door—a rasping sound
of sharp claws scratching against metal and the wail of a
creature that was neither human nor animal.

Perhaps the narrative voice is funny. Humorous
descriptions and focusing on the more ridiculous aspects of the story will give your narrative voice a fun,
breezy sound.

Melanie Ostrander never shut up. She talked during class (her teachers hated that), she talked during movies (her friends hated that), and she talked in her sleep (her older sister hated that). Melanie's mother even claimed that she heard Melanie talking while she was still in the womb, but Melanie's father said that it was just gas.

If you're not sure what personality your third-person narrative voice should have, don't stress. Begin telling the story and see what voice emerges. It may start off funny and gradually get more serious. You can always go back and edit to make it sound more consistent. Or you might want to leave it the way it is. There's nothing wrong with the tone of a narrative voice changing throughout the story, as long as there's a reason for the change (i.e., a story that starts out light and funny turns serious).

The Know-It-All: Third-Person Omniscient
by Ellen

This narrative is the all-powerful, all-knowing point of view. The narrator sees into everyone's brains all at once, and can skip from one character's point of view to another.

This is a really interesting narrative to use because you can explore the story from all different perspectives.

Here we go with an example.

Lily stared at the back of Shane's head, admiring the way he let his hair grow slightly too long and wondering if he was really listening to the droning voice of Mr. Kennedy.

He wasn't. In fact, he was wondering if Lily was staring at the back of his head, and hoping that the new dandruff shampoo was effective.

The Robo-Narrator: Third-Person Objective

by Ellen

In this narrative, the narrator doesn't see inside of anyone's brain. The narrator just describes what the characters do and say, without any emotion. Readers have to figure out what the characters are feeling through their dialogue and actions. Here's an example.

"Let me be," Jonah said. His face turned pale. He walked faster.

The big kid following behind him walked faster too. "Too late for that," he said. The big kid squinted up his dark eyes and clenched his hammy fists.

Okay, now that you know all the fancy terms for the different narratives and what they mean, you can have fun experimenting with them. Try writing your story with one narrative, say first person ("it's all about you"), then switch to another, for example, third-person omniscient ("the know it all"), and see which feels more comfortable. Or write a story weaving in several different narrative voices. Whenever I find myself stuck while writing a story, I go back and see if I need to change who's telling the story. A change of perspective can make all the difference in unsticking me. It lets me see the story with a fresh pair of eyes that may notice things that the first pair of eyes didn't. These new eyes may notice that the story isn't a gothic fantasy at all, but a wry spoof on one. Or they may notice that the swashbuckling pirate hero is actually a huge phony, and the real hero is an undersized cabin boy. Or the stern, uptight piano teacher may start belting out pop songs in the privacy of her bathroom.

How do you know when you hit on the right narrative voice? You'll feel it. Some writers experience a sort of spine-tingling sense of "rightness." Some writers want to dive right into the writing. All of a sudden your story will start to fall into place, and you'll know how to tell it.

I DARE YOU Take a story you have already written and rewrite it using a different narrative voice.

section

9

Starting Points

Boris the Bullet Boy:
Where to Start Your Story

by Ellen

Whenever I sit down to begin a new story, I get this hopped-up, jittery feeling—equal parts excitement and raw nerves. Anything can happen! Who knows what kind of trouble my characters are going to get themselves into? Who knows what sort of peculiar people or flesh-eating insects they might encounter? Ooo, I can't wait to begin . . .

The question is where to begin.

Not to make you nervous, but beginnings are pretty important. I'm sure you have picked up a book, read the first page, and put the book down again. Now it might be that the book just wasn't the sort of thing you like to read. But it also might be that the writer didn't create an enticing enough doorway into his or her world. Your opening sentences are your first crack at convincing your reader to keep turning the pages.

There are a few things I pay special attention to at the beginning of my books. For example, I like my character(s) to make a strong, definite entrance. I want my readers to know who they are dealing with right off the bat. They are going to be spending some time with these characters, and they need to feel invested in them right away.

Another thing I pay special attention to is the setting. My readers should get a good sense of where they are when they step into my fictional world. I want them to see the place, to taste it and smell it . . . and to decide that they'd like to stay for a while (for more about setting see "Chicken-Nugget Sky," in Section 10 on page 89).

As for where to begin, one good place to start is when your character is beginning something new. Just as you may feel an adrenaline rush when you begin your story, your character probably feels the same way starting a new school, moving into a new neighborhood, or learning how to dodge venom-tipped darts in the jungle. Starting with strong emotions and a situation in which anything can happen is a great way to pull your readers right into the story, like this:

Rodney Sloop stopped the car in front of the pair of rusted wrought-iron gates, and his younger brother Collin stared up at the sign that hung, lopsided, by a thick chain attached to the gate's spears. "McGnutch's Home for Unwanted Boys." Beyond the gate Collin could see a green building that was long and perfectly rectangular, as though a giant had chucked a giant-sized mossy brick over the gate. A smokestack was shoved into the top of the building, and sooty smoke shuddered out of it into the icy air.

"It's only for a little while," Rodney said without looking at his kid brother.

Collin nodded grimly, clutching the lumpy black Hefty bag to his belly.

"Just until I can find a job and a decent place to live in," Rodney added.

"In which to live," Collin said. When he was especially nervous, he corrected people's English. It made him feel a little braver, like the world really did have a certain logic to it, even when his own life had turned into a huge stinking mess.

Another good place to begin is in the middle of something. You can drop down right into the heart of a dramatic scene.

When Collin Sloop regained consciousness, he found himself slung over a beefy, freckled shoulder. From his upside-down vantage point, he could see a pair of green high-heeled shoes, and thickly muscled legs mincing their way through wooded underbrush. He groaned and tried to squirm off the shoulder, but a large hand swatted the back of his head.

"Stay put," the woman said.

"Who are you?" Collin asked weakly. His brain felt oddly muddled and slow moving.

"You call me Miss Trinka," the woman said in a deep sludgy accent. "And from now on you is being called Boris the Bullet Boy."

"Why?"

"Because we pay plenty money for you, Boris, so we call you what we like," Miss Trinka answered.

"But . . . where are you taking me?"

"To National Babatavian Traveling Circus. We is in much need of a human cannonball. The headmaster at your boys home say you have nice little puny head and big- gish kind of feet. Very astrodynamic."

"Aerodynamic," Collin said. He always corrected people's English when he was nervous. He earned another slap on the head for it.

"We'll see how smarty-pants you is when you is flying fifty feet in air in a cape and sparkly green tights!"

Or you can even begin at the end. Like this:

In the Babatavian Palace's elegant Great Room, the young princepessa sat cross-legged on a pile of red and blue cushions. She had a pointed nose and a pointed chin and was staring with pointed interest at the boy in the green helmet standing before her.

"You must remove your helmet in my presence," the princepessa commanded.

"Why?" the boy asked. He had a pale, plain, but clever face, and though he was wearing the most ridiculous costume—a sparkling green unitard with a lilac cape sewn onto the back—he still managed to look dignified. The princepessa briefly considered lying to him about palace protocol, but in the end decided to tell the truth.

"Because I want to see your puny head," she said.

The boy did not appear at all offended but he did sigh, as though he'd been asked to do this same thing too many times. He removed his helmet. His head was indeed puny. Satisfied, the princepessa gestured for Boris the Bullet Boy to take a seat beside her on the cushions.

"Now," she said, "you must tell me all about how you have come to be the greatest human cannonball in the history of the world."

Once you've decided where to start, how do you begin to tell the story? Sometimes it's tempting to stuff your opening paragraphs with lots of information. You may have a pretty clear idea about your characters and their situation and want to bring your readers up to speed. You may think it's a good idea to dump a truckload of facts about your characters on the first page. "Back her up, boys." Beep, beep. "Drop that load of back-story facts right there, in the first sentence."

Get a load of this:

As eleven-year-old Collin Sloop approached the front gate of the McGnutch's Home for Unwanted Boys, he thought about his poor parents who had died in a freak plane crash over the Amazon while they were on an archeological dig for the natural history museum. He thought about his old home in Chicago, where he used to be best friends with a boy named Poky. Poky's real name was Steve, but everyone called him Poky because one time someone yanked his pants down in the lunchroom and he was wearing polka-dot underwear. Collin turned around and glanced at his seventeen-year-old brother, Rodney, who was sitting in the car. Rodney was a part-time waiter who had his own band called The Incinerators. He had tried to take care of Collin on his own, but he was really selfish and immature, and he just couldn't hack it.

Whew! That's a honking big load of information! Your readers are going to get smothered under the weight of all that back-story. You can include all this information in your story, but slow down. Try and weave the information into your story in a more natural way. Your readers don't need to know every little thing right away. If your opening is strong enough, and your characters vivid enough, your readers will keep turning the pages, and they can find out about the plane crash on page six and the polka-dot underwear in chapter three.

Finally, don't give yourself a migraine trying to create the perfect beginning. Just start somewhere. After your story is finished, you can always go back and change it.

First Sentences: A Hand Reaches Up and Grabs You!

by Anne

Some people are patient readers. They can plod through paragraphs or pages, or even chapters, waiting for the action to get going. But I don't like to wait. I like to get involved in a book from the first sentence on. When I start a book, I want to feel as if a hand has reached up from the page and pulled me right inside the story.

I love first sentences that yank me into another world. Here are a few outstanding ones.

"When I was nine years old, I hid under a table and heard my sister kill a king."
— QUEST FOR A MAID, by Frances Mary Hendry

What? An older sister killing a king? And what about the nine-year-old crouched under a table? How does she feel about what her sister has done? Is she in danger? Is this a fairy tale or a story from another time? Who is the king, and why did she kill him? What I love about this first sentence is that it manages to be utterly simple and yet it raises so many questions that I just have to keep on reading.

"The daughter of a samurai does not scream when her hair is being combed."
— OF NIGHTINGALES THAT WEEP, by Katherine Paterson

I immediately know that I'm in Japan and that the heroine comes from a proud warrior family with a strict code of behavior. She is probably wealthy because someone else is combing her hair. Right from the start, there's a hint that she's going to rebel against her family or the code of honor. All this in only fourteen words. Katherine Paterson is a master.

"I thought that going to high school was going to be a big improvement over what I was used to."
— THE SNARKOUT BOYS AND THE AVOCADO OF DEATH, by Daniel Pinkwater

I'd read this book for the title alone. But I love the first sentence too. It's obvious that the narrator is about to be disappointed in a big way. Already I want to know—just how bad is it going to get? And what is he going to do about it?

"Freya awoke early and lay for a while in the dark, feeling her city shiver and sway beneath her as its powerful engines sent it skimming across the ice."
— PREDATOR'S GOLD, by Philip Reeve (from THE HUNGRY CITY CHRONICLES)

I'm in a world of shivering, swaying cities, but where girls still wake up in the morning and lie in the dark. This first sentence piques my curiosity and makes me trust the author. He's going to take me into a fantastic world, but there will be people who are like me, so I can experience it through their eyes.

Not all great books start off with a bang, but it's eye-opening to see the power of a single sentence. Pay attention to the kinds of opening sentences that send you tumbling into a new world, head first. And then try some of them yourself when you write your own story!

I DARE YOU Take any story idea and write a first sentence for it. Now try another first sentence. And another. Write until you have at least one zinger. It should make you desperately want to read more. (You might try it out on some friends.) It should also make you want to write more! Keep going.

If you don't have story ideas, you can just write irresistible first lines. Maybe you'll write such a tantalizing first sentence that you'll have to explore it in a story. It's happened to me!

section

10

How to Create a Great Story Setting

Adventures with Shoe-Box Dioramas

by Ellen

In elementary school my favorite teacher was Ms. Blau. She wore purple miniskirts and had a cute boyfriend who sometimes showed up at the end of the day. The best thing about Ms. Blau, though, was that if you hated writing book reports, she let you make shoe-box dioramas instead. I spent hours sitting on my bedroom floor, cutting up my father's green socks for grass, making trees out of toilet paper rolls and cotton balls, magic-markering tiny oak tag characters. When it was all done, I'd lie on my stomach and gaze into it, spellbound. It was just a box filled with bits of this and that, but all together it formed a miniature world; a world in which interesting things might happen.

Creating a setting for your story is not all that different from making a shoe-box diorama. You are piecing together a landscape with scraps. But instead of scraps of tinfoil or socks, you are using scraps of memory and imagination.

Chicken-Nugget Sky

by Ellen

As I mentioned earlier, I like to start my books with a very vivid setting. I do this, in part, because I need to hypnotize my readers into temporarily forgetting about the "real world" all around them, allowing them to enter into the "book's world." This is tricky. The real world is just so darn . . . real. That's why you have to make your setting at least as full of color, weather, shadows, plants, and smells as the real world. If this seems overwhelming, don't worry. You can start small. Really small.

Make a circle with your thumb and forefinger, about the size of a chicken nugget, and look through it. Aim it anywhere and you'll see a tiny sample of "setting." Right now, I'm aiming my circle at a coffee table where I can see a bit of a scented candle, my son's toy fire engine with one wheel missing, and a glob of slobber from the last time my American bulldog shook his head. That's setting. Even though it's chicken-nugget sized, it gives you an idea of what my world is like. You can begin to explore your story's setting the same way.

For example, if you want to start with the sky in your story, capture a bit of it in your chicken-nugget circle and have a good look at it (it doesn't have to be the actual sky above you, of course; it can be the sky in your mind's own private multiplex theater). Examine the color, the cloud formations, if there are any. Any smog? Planes? Dragons?

When you have a pretty clear picture of your story's sky, widen the chicken-nugget circle. Make it as big as a CD (imagine a movie camera that starts with a tight shot and gradually widens so that you can see the big picture). Can you see the tops of hills? Are they summer green or craggy from a hard winter? Or maybe you see buildings. Are they slim skyscrapers or the battered shingled roofs of a small town? Wider, now. Take your time. Let your setting reveal itself bit by bit and write down all the details. Details are a writer's best friend. They're the little buggers that help hypnotize our readers and keep them turning pages.

Mood Rings
by Ellen

Have you ever worn a mood ring? If you have, you might have noticed a curious thing: If you put it on when you're feeling just fine, and it turns black, you automatically start wondering if you are feeling rotten. You know, deep down.

Think of your story's setting as a mood ring. Writers want to make their readers feel a certain way— anxious, excited, gloomy—and setting is a way to subtly create a mood or a feeling deep down. Your reader may sit down with your story on a bleak winter's night, feeling rather glum (ring color: mud brown), but with carefully chosen descriptions, you can change his or her ring color pretty quickly.

Let's try and change our glum reader's ring color with an opening sentence:

The castle was bathed in sunlight, its majestic stones cloaked in spring-green ivy.

With just a few details, I've created a mood that is peaceful, calm, hopeful (this would turn our reader's mood ring a pleasant shade of blue, I think).

Now let's take that same castle and change the mood.

The castle was built with swamp-colored stones, its gaunt towers so tall they appear to scrape the dark, bruised sky.

Look out. Nasty, unpleasant stuff is on its way (uh-oh, the mood ring has definitely turned black).

Before you start writing a new scene, try and get a handle on the mood you want to create. As you are writing or when you are revising, choose your descriptive words carefully to build upon that mood. Setting is not just background. It's not just cardboard scenery. Setting is power. It's your chance, as a writer, to pull your readers in and rev up their emotion. You are in control. You choose the color of the ring.

I DARE YOU Write a scene about a circus, but make the mood dark and grim.

section

11

Suspense

The Cliff-. . . I mean Terrace-Hanger

by Ellen

One sweltering Saturday afternoon, when I was twelve
years old, I was sitting on my bedroom's windowsill with
my nose in a book. I don't remember what the book was,
but it must have been good because I hadn't come out my
room for hours. Just once I looked up from my book and
glanced out my window at the apartment building directly
across the street. Standing out on a terrace and watering
their grandmother's tomato plants were Iris and Yolanda
Diaz, the quiet and small-boned identical twins who went

to my school. They had large brown eyes with the sort of thick black lashes that you only see in little kids' drawings of princesses, and they often kept their hair in heavy, neat braids that reached all the way down their backs. Their grandmother took care of them, but she was so old and obese that it seemed to me the girls were really taking care of her. I often saw them hauling bags of laundry through the street or lugging groceries. Now I waved at them, and they smiled and waved shyly before ducking back inside.

I stuck my nose back in my book, vaguely aware of the sound of groaning traffic and, off in the distance, the haunting wail of sirens. With each passing moment the sirens grew louder. There seemed to be quite a lot of them, I noted. Still, that was no big deal . . . not in New York City during a heat wave. Crime always spiked during hot weather.

The wailing grew so loud now that I knew they were about to pass right by my building. Then, quite suddenly, the sirens stopped. The silence was eerie. Even the groaning traffic seemed to stop. I lifted my head out of my book and looked down at the street. Five police cars were lined up in front of Iris's and Yolanda's building. The police car doors were flung open, and the officers were gazing up at the building.

I looked up too and instantly sucked in my breath. A man was hanging from one of the outside terraces, seven stories above the ground. His hands were gripping the terrace's iron railing, and his legs were dangling in midair as he frantically tried to heave himself up to safety. I could see the taut squareness of his knuckles as he desperately tried to pull his weight upward. He raised his right leg, tilting dangerously to the left, then began a scooping motion with that leg, hoping to catch his heel on the terrace.

Had he tried to commit suicide then changed his mind? Had he leaned too far off the terrace railing and fallen?

Just then a woman rushed out onto the terrace below and began screaming and pointing up at the man hanging above her, "I've been robbed! That animal just broke into my apartment and robbed me!"

"Get back in your apartment and lock the terrace door!" one of the police ordered her through a bullhorn.

The woman scurried back into her apartment, and through the glass terrace door I could see her working the locks.

I looked back at the burglar. He had managed to pull himself up on the terrace and was now yanking hard on the terrace door to get into the next apartment. It was locked. For a moment it seemed like he didn't know what to do. He turned around and glanced down at the street full of cops, then over at my apartment building, and for one awful second I was positive he was looking directly at me. Even from that distance I could see how wild his eyes looked—frightened and desperate and capable of anything. I actually shrank back, as if he might leap across the street and pounce on me.

With sudden resolve, the burglar turned, jumped onto the terrace's top railing, and began to climb again.

It was then that I noticed two small faces looking out the window on the floor just above. Iris and Yolanda Diaz. Their identical dark eyes were calmly staring down at the police, curious as to what was happening. From their vantage point, I realized, they couldn't see the burglar, who had just now grabbed the railing of their terrace and was pulling himself up.

In a moment he would be at the Diaz's terrace door. Had they locked it after they watered the plants?

"Iris! Yolanda! Lock the terrace door!" I screamed out the window at them. But their window was shut—the air conditioner must be on, I thought—and they didn't hear me. I began to wave my arms at them to get their attention, but they didn't look my way.

My mind churned wildly, trying to think of something, anything, that could be done. I'll find their number in the phone book! I thought. I'll call them and warn them. But the next instant I realized that I didn't know their grandmother's name, and there would be dozens of Diaz's in the listings. There was nothing to do. I held my breath. My knuckles were pressed against my mouth. I watched, paralyzed. The burglar's foot caught the terrace. He hauled himself up. For a moment he paused. Caught his breath. Then he shoved past the tomato plants, knocking one down and shattering its pot as he headed for the terrace door....

Ha! I got you to keep reading! You want to know what happens next, right?

That's the power of suspense. We writers do have a few superhero-like powers up our sleeves, and one of them is the ability to make our readers turn a page, even when they know they should be doing their math homework or feeding their cat. We are able to do this in several ways: by creating interesting characters, by creating challenging situations for our interesting characters, and by creating moments of suspense.

Okay, I won't be a stinker and leave you hanging about the fate of Iris and Yolanda. Their terrace door was locked. The thief climbed another story to the roof of the apartment building where the police nabbed him in a matter of seconds. And yes, this is a true story . . . with a few embellishments to heighten the suspense.

Wait for It . . .

by Ellen

So how do you make your stories so suspenseful that your readers forget all about feeding their cat?

You have to prepare your readers for suspense. You can't just throw a suspenseful situation at them and expect them to be nibbling their nails with anticipation.

The first and best thing you can do to prepare your readers is to make sure you've created characters that they actually care about. In the short piece I wrote above, I tried to make Yolanda and Iris sympathetic (they really were very nice girls) so that the thought of a burglar entering their apartment would make you scared for them. It automatically raises the stakes.

Think about the book (or movie, if you haven't read the book) *Charlie and the Chocolate Factory*, by Roald Dahl. There are several characters in that book who want the same thing—the golden ticket that will allow them in the chocolate factory. Do we really care if spoiled Veruca Salt gets the ticket? Or piggy Augustus Gloop? Not much. But, oh . . . remember the moment when Charlie is opening that bar of chocolate sooo slowly, hoping with all his heart that the precious golden ticket is beneath that wrapper? We hope right along with him, holding our breaths, crossing our fingers, watching for that glint of gold. It's a beautiful moment of suspense. The reason we feel such suspense is that Charlie is a character we care about. He's a really decent kid who wants something very badly, and it is extremely hard for him to get it. This is his last chance, and if there is no golden ticket in that bar, he will probably be eating cabbage soup for the rest of his life. Ugh! The stakes are high, so the suspense is high.

And notice that this moment of suspense has nothing to do with scary stuff! You don't need imminent death or roaming werewolves to create a suspenseful moment. You just have to make your readers feel anxious about the outcome of the story's action.

Your choice of words also helps ramp up the suspense. As you are approaching your suspenseful situation, you can drop clues for the readers. In my piece I mention the haunting wail of police sirens in the distance and that the city's crime rate spikes during heat waves—two clues that something menacing might be coming down the pike. Dropping these clues is all about choosing your words carefully to create a certain atmosphere. If there is a werewolf (oh, what the heck, werewolves do make fun examples) roaming the woods through which your character is currently taking an evening stroll, you can write about fallen branches snapping beneath your character's shoes, like sparrows' bones. And of course, the full moon might be creeping in and out of sight, like a jaundiced, spying eye.

Finally, suspense works best when . . . wait for it . . . wait for it . . .

That's right. Suspense works best when you make your readers wait for the climax of the scene. This is the time for you to slow down and crank up the tension.

Have you ever had something really bad happen to you . . . even if it was just a supremely embarrassing moment? Did you notice how everything seemed to happen in slow motion? Did you notice how all your senses were heightened? That's the feeling you want to give to your readers in a suspenseful scene. Careful descriptions in moments of suspense can slow the pace and intensify your reader's anxiety. Make your readers smell the werewolf's decayed breath as he crouches beside an oak tree. Make them see the white flash of his incisors as his glistening lips draw back.

You can play with the rhythms of your sentences too. Shorter sentences can slow down the pace of the scene. Shorter sentences can also bring to mind the sound of hesitant footsteps gradually—maybe fearfully—approaching something. Like this:

She sniffed the air. Her eyebrows cinched together. There was an unsettling odor. Wet dog, maybe? Yes. But something else too. Something feverish.

A series of very short sentences can even make your readers think of the beating of a heart.

There was a growl. Low. Deep. Eager.

Longer sentences can be useful too. They can give your readers a breathless sensation. You can use them to quicken the pace at key moments and give your scene a frantic feeling. Let's give it a try.

She began to run. The branches tore at her bare arms and legs, and the cold air pinched her lungs, but the sound of footsteps behind her—terrifyingly agile and soft as a panther's—kept her moving despite the pain, despite the gnawing sense that it was utterly hopeless.

Can you hear her breathing hard? I can.

Phew! All this suspense is making me jittery. I'm going to take a nice calm bath. Then maybe I'll feed the cat.

I DARE YOU Think of an ordinary event that you wouldn't consider suspenseful. It might be waiting for the school bus, walking your dog, or visiting your grandparents. Create a situation in which this everyday event suddenly becomes incredibly suspenseful.

Title Tattle

A Few Measly Words

by Ellen

Titles are just a few measly words strung together. No big deal. So why is it so tricky to find a good title for your story?

Well, to be fair, it's not always hard. Some titles just step up, fling their arms wide, and declare, "Look no further, my friend! I am, indisputably, the perfect title for your story!"

I love when that happens.

More often than not, though, you will have to rummage around for a good title. There are always several titles that might work, but don't be hasty in choosing one. Do you ever pick up a book in a store simply because the title intrigues you? I do. Your title is your reader's first impression of your story. As a writer, you have to decide what sort of first impression you are going for.

Choosing a title for this book was really tough. Anne and I spent weeks bouncing titles back and forth. Here's a sample of our cell phone conversations.

Anne: Hey, Ellen. I'm taking a walk right now, and I was thinking . . .

Ellen: You're taking a walk in a snow storm?

Anne: I have good boots on. Anyway, I was thinking—

Ellen: Okay, but don't slip.

Anne: I won't. So I was thinking about a title for our book. What do you think of "The Three-Hundred-Pound Draft"?

Ellen: Oooo. I like it. But . . .

Anne: But?

Ellen: It sounds a little intimidating.

Anne: Yeah, I see your point.

OR

Ellen: Hey, Anne. Okay, Ian's busy putting diapers on the dog, so I can talk. What do you think of this title . . . oh, wait. Hold on. (Background sounds of barking and a little boy's voice saying, "Keep still, Otto! Your tail is caught in the leg hole!")

Anne: You sure you can talk now?

Ellen: Yeah, yeah, it's fine. Ian's busy buttering his own head now. . . . So, what do you think of "Chicken-Nugget Sky" as a title?

Anne: Hmm.

Ellen: You don't like it?

Anne: Well, chicken nuggets? I mean, they are pretty gross.

Ellen: Yeah, I see your point.

We went through loads of other titles too. Here are just a few of them: "Stalking the Wild Character," "Writing From the Inside Out," "A Rage for the Page," "Writing Wild," "Rebel Writers," "Page Rage," and "Anne and Ellen's Book of Writing Advice."

In the end we chose *Spilling Ink*. We wanted the book to appeal to all kids, even the ones who would run screaming at the mere mention of a book about writing. The title *Spilling Ink* sounded fun and slightly rebellious.

You could tell it was a writing book because of the ink, but it didn't sound like a boring textbook on writing.

Here are a few pointers for title rummaging.

1. Don't panic if you can't think of a title while you're writing your story. Many times writers don't find a good title until after the story is finished.

2. On the other hand, you might be the sort of writer who likes to start writing with a title in mind. It can help you stay focused on what the story is going to be about. If that's the case, you can start with a "working title," which is sort of like a temporary title. You might wind up keeping it, or you might decide to change it when the story is finished.

3. Reread your story and see if anything jumps out at you. It might be a single word or a phrase that sums up some important element in your story. I recently did this for my book *SLOB*, because the word plays such a pivotal role in the story.

4. Make a list of objects that play a significant role in your story, for instance:
   a) faded quilt
   b) shattered window
   c) portrait of dead Uncle Marvin

See if any of the objects could also be symbolic for a theme in your story. If, for instance, your story is about a

family's history, "Portrait of Dead Uncle Marvin" might make a good title.

5. You can try to sum up the main idea of your story in the title. I like to fiddle around with words to make the title sort of snappy. For instance, if your story revolves around an eight-year-old boy who is so awful to his two-year-old brother that he is magically transformed into the toddler's servant, you might title it "Fairy Godbrother" or "Baby Butler."

6. You can use the name of your main character, like *Pippi Longstocking*. Still, just titling your story

"Sarah" might not be interesting enough to draw in your reader. Using a name for a title works well when the character's name is a little unusual or when you have something else in the title that makes the name pop, like *Sarah, Plain and Tall*.

7. You can use the name of an important place in your story for the title, like *The Chronicles of Narnia*.

8. Have a trusted friend read your story and see if he or she can brainstorm titles with you.

9. When you think you may have found a title you like, double-check to see if it gives the right first impression of your story. If your story is dark and grim and your title is funny, your readers are going to expect a few chuckles. People hate to not chuckle when they are all set to chuckle. It's like holding up your hand for a high five and not getting one.

Check that you like the title's sound. Say it out loud a few times. Then say: "I read this great story the other day called [insert your title]. I can't stop thinking about it. Have you read [insert your title]? Oh, you should. I think everyone should read [insert your title]."

If that sounds good to you, the title is probably a keeper.

How to Write Dialogue

Blabbedy-Blab

by Ellen

A lot of what we say to each other every day is
blabbedy-blab.

"Hey! What's up?"

"Nothing. What's up with you?"

"Not much."

"All right. See you later."

"Yup. Later."

See what I mean? Blabbedy-blab. There's nothing

wrong with blabbedy-blab in real life. We're just making conversation and trying to connect with each other.

Fiction dialogue, however, should aim a little higher than blabbedy-blab.

When I was pregnant with my son, I read all kinds of pregnancy books to find out what I should and shouldn't be eating. Many of the books warned that just because you were eating for two, you shouldn't scarf down Twinkies and cheeseburgers. They were just empty calories. Instead, you should eat the substantial stuff, with vitamins and protein and that sort of thing. You should make every bite count.

The same goes for dialogue. You don't want to fill up your story with empty dialogue, like "How are you?" "Fine, thanks." That's Twinkie dialogue. Instead, fill up your story with the substantial stuff, making every little morsel count. Let your dialogue contain words that anger your characters or soothe them, intrigue them, or change their life.

Let your dialogue be a mouth-watering lasagna with buttered carrots on the side. And okay, maybe a slice of devil's food cake for dessert. A small one.

Walk the Talk: Revealing Your Character Through Dialogue

by Ellen

A few lines of good dialogue can reveal more about your characters than an entire page of description. It can tell your readers how old the characters are, how they feel about what is happening in the scene, what part of the country (or world or galaxy) they come from, if they are outspoken or shy, mean-spirited or kind. With dialogue, your characters can tell bold-faced lies, or they can whisper secrets, conceal fears, or admit to them. Dialogue is one of your most powerful tools, so let it work for you. Use it to move your story along, show the readers what your characters are made of, and deepen the drama.

Consider this bit of dialogue.

"Excuse me, sir, but I think you may be wrong about the Hydro-Tectonic Theory," Kurt said.

Now that's just one line of dialogue, but already the reader can tell several things about Kurt. He is probably smart, since he is correcting someone who seems to be an authority on the subject of the Hydro-Tectonic Theory. He is also polite—we get this from the "Excuse me, sir" part—but he's bold enough to contradict the person in authority. However, even though he's bold and probably smart, he's not arrogant. We know this because he says, "I think you may be wrong . . ." instead of "you are wrong."

Let's go on with this example.

"Is that so, Kurt?" Mr. Wellington said. "Well, stand up and tell the class why you think I don't know what I'm talking about. Oh, but before you do, you should probably zipper your fly."

Hmmm. Mr. Wellington is a bit of a stinker. In his three lines of dialogue, we can see he is offended by Kurt's questioning of his knowledge. He seems insecure too because he says, "tell the class why you think I don't know what I'm talking about." Lastly, Mr. Wellington hits below the belt. Literally. He has no problem humiliating Kurt by telling the class that Kurt's fly is open.

Oh, and the fact that Kurt's fly is open may indicate that Kurt is a little absentminded.

With just four lines of dialogue, we've discovered a few important things about the characters. Not only that, but some dramatic tension has been created. It's Kurt versus Mr. Wellington. Kurt is going to have to zipper his fly in front of the whole class. Then he will either stand up and say why he thinks Mr. Wellington is wrong (making

Mr. Wellington even more furious) or he will back down and say nothing. Personally, I'm curious as to what he will do.

Now don't fuss over every little line of dialogue when writing the first draft of your story. Save the fussing for your revision. When writing your first draft, let your characters speak their minds. Just let the words flow out of their mouths and try to hear their speech rhythms and slang and hesitations. Get very familiar with the way they speak without forcing words into their mouths. When you go back and revise your story, sift through the dialogue more carefully and see if you can sharpen it so that the dialogue reveals more about the characters and helps the story move forward.

"So Here's What Happened . . ."

by Ellen

You can use dialogue to give behind-the-scenes information in the story. Let's say your main character wasn't allowed to go to a party that her best friend went to. Let's also say that something important happened at that party, and you want your reader to know about it. You can have the best friend describe what happened in an exchange of dialogue with the main character. Just keep in mind that when behind-the-scenes information is described in dialogue, it doesn't have that power-punch impact of "seeing" it happen directly. If you use this technique, try to focus on the characters who are talking, not just the information being given, in order to keep the drama front and center. Bring the readers' attention to the characters' body language and their reactions to the information.

Like this:

"Was Jared at the party?" Lucy asked as they sat by the edge of the pool.

Melissa suddenly slipped into the water and began swimming laps. Lucy paused for a few minutes, squinting at her friend suspiciously before she picked up an inflatable turtle and slapped it on Melissa's head as she came up for air.

"Hey, what was that for?" Melissa said.

"I asked you a question."

"Yes, Jared was there," Melissa said. She grabbed the inflatable turtle and hugged it to her chest as though bracing herself for the next question.

"Was he alone?" Lucy asked.

"Not exactly."

"Arianna?" Lucy asked. She said the name the way a patient says to her doctor, "Cancer?"

"Sorry, Lucy," Melissa said diving beneath the water again.

In this scene I kept the drama in the present moment rather than just rehashing what happened at the party. Lucy's and Melissa's body language—and the inflatable turtle—tell the real story about what happened at the party.

He Said, She Said

by Ellen

Things like "he snarled" and "she shouted" at the end of your dialogue are called noisy tag lines. Well, that's not their official name; it's just what I call them. With noisy tag lines, characters are snapping, crying, yelling, hissing, snarling, growling, wailing, or shrieking. It sounds like an afternoon at the zoo. Many writing books say you should avoid using noisy tag lines. They say that writers should be able to express these emotions in the dialogue itself, and just a plain "he said" or "she said" should be enough in most cases. They have a good point. What often happens in dialogue is that readers mentally skip over the "he said/ she said" part and just read the dialogue itself. This gives the dialogue a nice, natural flow. Using the noisy tag lines makes the tag line pop out, which can be distracting to readers, pulling their focus away from the dialogue.

Still, I'm not a fan of "you shouldn't" rules when it comes to writing. Some of the world's finest writers were incorrigible rule breakers. I think it's fine to break rules, so long as you know what the rules are and you are breaking them for a good reason.

Here are a few things to keep in mind about noisy tag lines.

1. When you want to use a noisy tag line, first check and see if you really need it, for instance:

   "I hate this stupid camp!" Jennifer cried.

   Can you hear the sound of annoyance in Jennifer's voice? It's clear from what she says and the exclamation point that she's pretty upset. You don't really need to use *cried* because you can hear it in the dialogue.

2. Too many noisy tag lines all clumped together makes for too much noise. Look at this example:

   "Leave my hair alone," he snarled.
   "But it looks nice all fluffy," she squealed.
   "Next time you touch my hair, I'll take your comb and throw it out the window," he snapped.
   "But I just want to put a little mousse in it," she wailed.

That's an awful lot of snapping and squealing and wailing. It might be hard for your readers to concentrate on the story with all that noise.

3. Consider if you actually need a tag line at all. When you have a long passage filled with dialogue, you don't need to add tag lines to every line of dialogue if it's obvious who is speaking. For instance:

"You lied to me," Ben said.

"I had to," said the dragon.

"But I trusted you."

"Never trust a dragon."

"Why not?"

"Because we have nine-inch talons and fire coming out of our mouths! For heaven's sake, kid, grow up."

"The odds don't look too good for that, though, do they?"

"Nope. Not good at all."

Occasionally eliminating tag lines can give your dialogue a great flow. It also gives the dialogue a quicker pace, which can be useful in tension-filled scenes.

4. Double-check that your noisy tag line makes sense. Think about this one:

"You are disgusting!" she laughed.

It's hard to laugh and talk at the same time. The words come out all funny. Try it.

5. You may actually want a noisy scene with lots of snarling and snapping. In that case, try and use some noisy tag lines, but take care not to use too many. A few well-chosen shrieks or wails can ratchet up the drama in a scene.

Adverbial Tag Lines

by Ellen

This is fancy term for something you have seen thousands of times. Adverbial tag lines are simply when an adverb is attached to a tag line. Here are some examples.

"I hope my mother doesn't embarrass me," Brian said cheerfully ("said cheerfully" is the adverbial tag line).

"That shade of green makes you look like a zucchini," Alana said rudely ("said rudely" is the adverbial tag line).

Like noisy tag lines, adverbial tag lines should enhance the dialogue in some way. In the second example, it doesn't. It's obvious that what Alana said was rude, so the adverbial tag line, "Alana said rudely" adds absolutely nothing to the dialogue. If I were you, I'd scrap it. Actually I'm the one who wrote it, so since I am me, I'll scrap it.

The first example, however, does add something to the dialogue. If you read the line of dialogue without the tag line, you would probably assume that Brian was nervous about his mother embarrassing him. You might imagine his voice sounding anxious or distressed. Yet the tag line says he is cheerful. That adds an unexpected layer to the dialogue.

Try and use adverbial tag lines sparingly and only when they can shed light on something that the dialogue can't.

Writers' Rules to Ignore or Adore? Kill the "Interesting" Words

by Anne

Many years ago, I attended a writers' group as a guest author. One of the women read a long, plainly written piece. I can't remember much about it, but it might have gone something like this:

The boy slid down the slope and said, "I'd like to do that again, please."

"You can't," said his mother. "It's time for dinner."

"Okay, Mom," the boy said.

When she had finished reading, the leader of the group noted that her story needed more excitement. She told her to "use more interesting words" when she revised.

"And don't use the word *said* so much," she added.

I gasped in horror, as only a professional writer would.

The story was kind of boring, but the group leader's solution was terrible. Let's take a look at why. First, as an experiment, we'll get rid of the word *said*.

The boy scampered down the slope and whined, "I'd like to do that again, please."

"You can't," his mother admonished, "it's time for dinner."

"Okay, Mom," the boy chortled.

When a word means something, use it. For example, *whined* works nicely in the first sentence. The word *pleaded* would also work.

But *said* sounds so much better than admonished and chortled. Those two words, in this story, are silly and pretentious.

There's nothing wrong with the word *said*. Some people think it's too plain, but I think they're wrong. Said is a good, honest, workmanlike word. It will serve you well in hundreds of situations. When you can't think of another word, said will always do the job. Never be ashamed of using it.

Here are more ways to ruin your writing with "interesting" words.

The boy slid crazily down the jagged, muddy slope and snarled loudly, "I'd like to do that again, please."

"You can't," his accepting mother hissed in a ragged tone of voice. "It's time for dinner."

"Okay, Mom," the boy howled resentfully.

This version is more entertaining. But can you imagine reading an entire book like this? You'd need a plunger to get through the clogged prose.

So how would I make this story more interesting? The classic method is to concentrate on characters and action. If they aren't interesting, no fancy words will ever make your story right. So let's see what we can do to the boring story. Here are a couple of rewrites.

He didn't want to go home. He knew what was waiting there. When his mother appeared in her dark, shapeless winter coat, he pretended not to see her.

He slid down the slope again.

"Michael," his mother called.

"I'm going down again," he said. "One more time."

"But it's time for dinner," she said. She looked as if she were about to cry. There was a bandage wrapped around her hand.

He wanted to say no, but he couldn't. He couldn't leave her alone. Slowly he got up and brushed the snow from his knees. "Okay, Ma," he said.

Did that grab your interest? I hope so. Here's another take.

It was the best sledding hill in town, and it was packed. There were dozens of kids here today. Everyone had a sled or a toboggan or even a piece of a cardboard.

He trudged up the hill, pulling his old sled behind him. His face stung from the cold, but he was happier than he had been in months. All day long, he had been sledding. And finally, the kids who had ignored him ever since he moved here last fall had begun to say hello to him.

He never wanted this day to end.

But there was his mother, at the bottom of the hill, impatiently jiggling the car keys.

He jumped on his sled for one last ride down the slope. Snow flew in his face. As he zoomed downhill, he yelled at the top of his lungs. Some of the other kids were calling to him, urging him on.

"Go, Michael!" they shouted.

The sound of his name was sweet. He wanted to hear it again and again. He came to a perfect stop in front of his mother. "Please, Mom? Just one more time?"

But she was already walking to the car. She didn't even hear him. She probably thought he was glad to leave. He stood up and brushed the snow from his knees.

"Okay, Mom," the boy said. "I'll go home with you now. But I'm coming back tomorrow."

I DARE YOU Write your own version of the boring story!

Don't Just Stand There Yapping . . . Do Something!

by Ellen

Watch people when they speak. It's not just their mouths that are moving. Their hands may be waving around, their eyebrows raising, their foot tapping. Body language is powerful stuff because it's often done unconsciously. (Why do you think the FBI hires body language specialists to help determine when someone is lying?) In fiction writing, pairing action with words is a good way to strengthen the impact of your dialogue and break the monotony of long stretches of dialogue.

Here are a few ways to do this.

1. You can use an action instead of a tag line when you want to reinforce what your character is saying with a visual. An example would be:

   "This is really hard for me to say to you." Robert looked away while he gnawed at his thumbnail.

   Or you can use it with a tag line. Here goes:

   "There has got to be a toilet somewhere in this mall," Anna said, walking swiftly with an anxious look in her eye.

2. You can use it to show that your character is being less than truthful:

   "Tell me the truth, Todd. How bad is the wound on my leg?" Ron asked.
   "Lie still, I'll take a look." With his back turned to Ron, he rolled up Ron's pant leg, then grimaced with horror. "It's not that bad," he said.

This is interesting because the reader is in on the lie, while the character being lied to may be clueless. You can also have a character lie in a more subtle way so that the reader suspects that a character may be lying but isn't sure. Many mystery books use this technique. An example:

"How well did you know the victim?" the detective asked.
"Oh, I hardly knew him at all," Mrs. Biddle replied, her fingers toying worriedly at a tangle in her Yorkshire terrier's hair.

Are her fingers "toying worriedly" because she is worried about her little dog's hair or because she is worried about being accused of murder? Hard to tell, and it plants a seed of suspicion in the reader's mind (I'm constantly amazed at the power of a few well-placed words).

3. Action can be used to break up the monotony of a long string of dialogue. Next time you open a book, notice how you read when you come to a section with a lot of dialogue, especially one in which there are few tag lines. There's a back-and-

forth, watching-a-Ping-Pong-game rhythm. Blip-blop, blip-blop, blip-blop. It can be almost hypnotic in its flow, which is a cool effect.

However, if the writer inserts some action into the dialogue, two things will happen: One, it will create a pause in the action, like when one of the players misses the Ping-Pong ball and it rolls off the table. Everything stops for a moment. The reader is pulled out of the "dialogue trance." And two, the action really pops out as something significant. That's why you should choose the action carefully when you use this technique. The action should give the readers an important bit of information about either the character or the situation. Here's an example.

"I can't; I won't!" Justine said, her hands flying up to cover her neck.
"But think of all the advantages," the vampire said.
"Like what?"
"You'll live forever."
"And watch all the people I love grow old and die?"
"You can meet new people."
"And suck out their blood."
"There's another advantage too."
"Forget it. My mind is made up."

"Just listen."

"No!"

"Your skin will look great. You'll never get another zit."

"Really?" Justine's hands slowly moved away from her neck. "Not even if I eat chocolate?"

Did you see how Justine "missed the Ping-Pong ball" in the last line of dialogue by moving her hand away from her neck? It stops the momentum of the argument, and it points out that something new has just happened—she is rethinking the idea of becoming a vampire. The gesture is important too, since she is suddenly no longer protecting her jugular vein from a thirsty blood-sucker. Well, honestly . . . imagine an eternal zitless, chocolate-filled existence. Can you blame the poor girl?

I DARE YOU Write a scene in which one character tries to tell another character something, but can't. Think about the ways a character might circle around the topic and hint at things without saying them outright. Include body language that helps reveal the character's secret thoughts.

I DOUBLE DARE YOU Write a scene in which one character is trying to convince another character to do something he or she doesn't want to do, using only dialogue.

Description

Competing with Smooshed Toads

by Ellen

When I was a kid, I loved Laura Ingalls Wilder's
Little House series. The part that always shocked me,
no matter how many times I read it, was when Laura's
sister, Mary, went blind. Poor beautiful, goody-two-shoes
Mary! Yes, sometimes you wanted to slap her for being
such a know-it-all, but you didn't want her to go blind
for goodness' sake! Their father told Laura that since
Mary was blind, Laura would have to be her sister's eyes.
She'd have to describe the world around her in detail so

that Mary could "see it" as clearly as Laura did. So that's exactly what Laura did. When the family took their first ride in a train, Laura described every little detail to her sister, from the red velvet seats to the shiny brass buttons on the conductor's coat, until Mary could see the train perfectly in her own mind, even though she had never been in one before.

As a writer, you have to be your readers' eyes. When they first pick up your story, your readers are totally blind and helpless. They don't know if they are standing in a grimy Laundromat or the pink-walled office of the pink-faced principal or on the surface of a wind-swept planet with bubbling, mucuslike puddles underfoot. If you don't bother to describe your fictional world to your readers, or you rush through your descriptions quickly and carelessly, it's likely that your readers will stumble around in this strange, shadowy place until they finally say, "Oh, forget it! I can't see a thing in this story! I'm going outside to have a look at that smooshed toad on the sidewalk."

Here are some things to keep in mind when you are writing description.

    1. Take your time. Don't rush through descriptions so that you can get back to the action. Good descriptions will make your characters' actions

more powerful. Say one of your characters is a farm boy whose dream is to win a brand-new John Deere tractor for his father by competing in a local sheep-shearing competition. If you take the time to describe just how rusted and dented his father's own tractor is, the awful belching sounds it makes when his father tries to get it started, and how his father's room is plastered with torn-out magazine photos of sleek green and yellow John Deere tractors, your character's efforts to win that competition will carry a much bigger punch.

2. If you are trying to describe something that really exists, you can take a little field trip to "stop and notice" it. For instance, if you are writing about a town based on the one you live in, take a walk around and look at the town as though you have never seen it before. (Hint: Wear a pair of sunglasses if you don't want people to know that you are staring. Also, it will make you feel like a spy, which is always nice.) Maybe you'll notice that the houses on the east side of town are all freshly painted, but the neighborhood is as quiet as a crypt, while the weather-beaten old houses on the west side have loads of kids laughing and screeching on the streets outside of them. Or you might

notice a mysterious message taped to someone's front door that says, "Emmaline, meet me in the igloo at midnight." In any case, by the time you sit back down to write your story, you will be able to describe that town in a much more colorful way than you would have before your field trip.

If you are basing one of your characters on someone you know, begin to pay special attention to him or her (the sunglasses trick might come in handy here too). Take notes, jotting down any-thing you observe: "A second before she drinks her juice, her tongue pokes into her glass." "Her sneakers always look clean. Does she wash them every day?" "She sounds like a nervous sheep when she laughs."

3. Most writers work from a mixture of the real and the imagined. You can take field trips inside your own brain too. Close your eyes and "see" the thing you are trying to describe—all its colors and shapes and smells and things you might compare it to (see "Metaphors and Similes" in Section 15 on page 144). Skip over the descriptions that you've heard before, like "eyes as blue as the sky," and dig a little deeper. See if you can find a more original description, something that is entirely

your own but still perfectly true. Maybe his eyes are the blue of the shadows on hummocks of snow. Or maybe they are as blue as the china bowl that his mother kept locked in her glass cabinet. Or the blue of a poison dart frog.

4. I tend to use a lot of description at the beginning of my books. Remember, that's when your readers are the most blind and helpless. Starting off with vivid descriptions of setting and character helps your readers get their bearings. You'll gain their trust right away. They'll know that you will be their eyes for them, and that your eyesight is as sharp as a hawk's. Trust me, they'll forget all about that smooshed toad on the sidewalk.

5. Don't stress about thinking up fancy descriptions. You don't have to know all sorts of complicated, sophisticated words in order to describe things well. Keep it simple, if that's your style. If a person has red cheeks, you don't have to write, "the crimson-colored blush on his snowy skin made it look as though he'd been slapped by a January mistral in the North Pole." Really, you can just write that his cheeks were red. That will do just fine. And anyway, I don't think mistrals blow in the North Pole.

6. On the other hand, if you are the sort of writer who just loves fancy descriptions, that's great too. Pull out all those juicy adjectives from the thesaurus and festoon your story with them. Drape them over your nouns so that they are spangled, plumed, bejeweled, and bedazzling. I have just one word of warning: Make sure that your love of fancy description doesn't become more important than your characters and what they are doing. Pages and pages of description without any action can get boring pretty fast, and a glittering adjective palace does nothing for your story if the characters who live in it are as boring as a bowl of cornmeal mush. Remember, characters and their desires always come first. Always, always, always.

I DARE YOU Describe the color yellow to someone who cannot see. You won't be able to say things like "the color of a dandelion" since that person wouldn't know what you were talking about. Instead, you'll have to get really creative and think about what the color yellow reminds you of. If it had a smell, what would it be? What would it sound like, taste like, feel like? How does it make you feel? Make that person "see" yellow. I promise you, you'll never think of yellow the same way afterward.

Writers' Rule to Ignore or Adore?
The Rule of Three

by Anne

Here's a writers' rule that may help you write description. I learned about the rule of three when I was starting out. It really stuck in my head, and I always remembered it as I wrote.

To use the rule of three, you employ three adjectives in a description, or have a person do three actions, or have a dialogue of three parts. You can use it to describe a person, place, or scene. It's supposed to make any action or speech feel more complete.

For example, when I was writing about a boy, I wouldn't describe him as "skinny as a ferret with a red, twitching nose." I'd describe him as "skinny as a ferret, with a red, twitching nose, and a mouth that always gaped open."

After a while, I began to question this rule. Why three? Why not fewer or more? Did I have to do it with every single description or action?

Okay, let's check this out scientifically. Which do you prefer?

She ate only lamb chops, had a chronic lisp, and wore a nose ring.

OR

She ate only lamp chops and had a chronic lisp.

He came into the room, perched on the armoire, and began to saw off his pant cuffs.

OR

He came into the room and began to saw off his pant cuffs.

"I really loathe eighth grade," Jessica said, tossing her hamburger into the trash.

"Only twenty students have gotten food poisoning this year," Percival pointed out.

"Twenty-seven," Jessica corrected him.

"A record low," Percival said.

"I want another hamburger," Jessica said. "Do you have two dollars?"

"If you don't mind it in pennies," Percival said, pulling a small bank out of his backpack.

OR

"I really loathe eighth grade," Jessica said, tossing her hamburger into the trash.

"Only twenty students have gotten food poisoning this year," Percival pointed out.

"Twenty-seven," Jessica corrected him.

"A record low," Percival said.

Both versions works well—depending on what you want. If the rule of three helps you, use it, but you might just prefer no rules at all.

More Crawling Lizards, Please: Talking About Illustrations

Picturing Books

by Anne

Want to write a picture book? It's not that different from writing a story or novel, except:

It's only about thirty-two pages, with a few words or lines on each page.

There are pictures.

Your readers are often younger than five years old. You have to keep things very simple.

Seems pretty easy, huh? But like all other types of writing, you may find yourself getting stuck along the way. In case you do, here are a few more tips on writing picture books.

When you write a picture book, it helps to break it down into pages. See each page almost as a separate chapter (in only a few words!). Each page should advance the story or reveal a new aspect of it. Even though I don't illustrate my own books, while I'm writing I always imagine a picture for each page. Then I write words to accompany the imagined scene. What I see in my mind is never anything like the finished artwork. Once I lay eyes on the actual illustrations, my own images vanish forever. No matter how hard I try to remember, they never come back.

A picture book can be written entirely in pictures. If you love to draw as much as you love to write, you might try that sometime. Or you might team up with a friend as your artist.

Kids are often surprised to hear that I've never met the artists who illustrate my picture books. In fact, I never speak to any of them until the book is finished. Contrary to what you might think, a writer doesn't dictate to the illustrator. I wouldn't want someone telling me how to write, so I don't tell an artist how to draw. He should be free to develop his imagination and vision of my story the way he wants. Of course, I make comments on the pictures when they're done, and sometimes the artist will make a few changes. I've always had wonderful artists for all my books.

When you write a picture book, it's also very important to remember your readers, who are usually much younger than you are. In fact, they probably won't even be reading the book themselves! Someone will be reading it to them.

So how do you write for someone who's a different age than you? I think of it as being in two places at once, or being two people at the same time. If I'm writing a picture book, I put myself into the mind of a five-year-old. I see and experience the world as the five-year-old. (It helps if you know someone that age and have observed that child carefully!) But I never lose my real self; I'm also seeing the world through my own eyes, as well as the five-year-old's eyes. It's like having two streams of thought going on simultaneously. Or like being one of those wooden dolls with many dolls inside it.

If you're writing for a very young child, you will want your story to feel comforting and complete by the end. I love picture books that are like circles. They set out from home, go around the world on a grand adventure, and then return safely back home to be tucked into bed by their mother.

I DARE YOU Either alone or with a friend, write a picture book. Imagine the kind of book you would like to read to a little sister or brother, or to a small child you know. Make yourself a book with folded paper and number the pages. Then write your story, imagining— or drawing—an illustration on each page. When you're done, you can give it to a friend to illustrate, if you want. Then read it to a small child. Does that change how you see your story? Revise it, if you wish.

Working with Illustrators

by Ellen

It's always fun—and shocking—to see how an illustrator imagines scenes and characters from your book. It's often far different from what you imagined . . . and many times it's better.

When I first saw Peter Reynolds' illustration of my character Olivia Kidney, I smiled in amazement. I had never really described her physically in the book. To be honest, I wasn't entirely sure what she looked like. I knew her mind and heart, but I hadn't thought very much about her hair color or the shape of her eyes.

When I saw Peter's illustrations of Olivia though, with her disheveled dark hair and lanky body, I knew that was exactly what she looked like!

People often ask me, "How closely do writers work with illustrators?" The answer is, it depends. Anne, for instance, didn't talk to the illustrators of her books until the book was done. Peter Reynolds, on the other hand, checked in with me often as he worked. He would e-mail his rough drafts to me, and I would make comments like, "I think Olivia's dad should be more goofy-looking," or "There needs to be more lizards crawling on the woman's shoulders," or more often than not, "It's perfect!"

Since Olivia Kidney was loosely set in the apartment building in which I grew up, Peter Reynolds requested that I send him photos of my childhood home, then he worked off those photos. I loved that! It was like a special secret in the book.

Two Secret Artists

Not many people know this, but both Anne and I started off as artists, and then switched to writing. I still find that the art background comes in handy. When a character has me stumped, I'll occasionally make sketches of him or her. Seeing the worried expression

in the character's eyes or the way the person crosses his or her arms stubbornly can give me insight into the character's personality. I've also mapped out buildings or towns and drawn several of the oddball inventions from my book *SLOB*.

Unlike me, Anne doesn't draw her characters, but some of her characters like to draw. Artists and art often show up in her books, and Anne tells me that her imagination is very visual. She likes to "see" her stories as she writes them.

Still, neither Anne nor I have ever really been seriously tempted to illustrate our own books. A good illustrator brings a pair of fresh, creative eyes to your words and can give your readers a deeper understanding of your story. For instance, I'd always pictured Olivia Kidney as a tough, sarcastic city kid, but Peter's drawings showed another side of her too. She looked young and vulnerable and a bit baffled at all the strange people she was encountering. It gave Olivia, and the whole story, an extra dimension.

In any case, my ancient oil paint tubes are quite rusty, and so are my art skills, I'm afraid.

section 16

Shape Shifters

Metaphors and Similes

by Ellen

Presto-Change-o! Metaphors

I really love metaphors because they allow you to play with your reader's head. In a good way, I mean.

A metaphor sounds kind of fancy and complicated, but it really isn't. I bet you use metaphors all the time. When was the last time you compared two things that seemed to have little in common, without using the word like or as? Have you ever said, "I'm boiling mad" or "I was frozen with fear"? How about, "I just had a brain fart." There. You used a metaphor, and you didn't even know it.

In a story, a good metaphor allows your reader to see something in a totally new way. Think of a metaphor as a magic spell that allows an object to shape-shift. Say the magic metaphoric words and poof! That object instantly turns into its secret, hidden characteristic.

Here's an example.

Mr. Straus lumbered over to Ryan, clamped his hairy paw on Ryan's shoulder, and growled in his ear, "Give me an example of a metaphor."

"Um, my memory is pretty cloudy, Mr. Straus," Ryan said.

"Excellent," Mr. Straus grunted bearishly before his small predatory eyes searched for another terrified student to pounce upon.

With this metaphor, Mr. Straus has shape-shifted into a bear. Of course your reader understands that Mr. Straus is a man not a bear, but the metaphor has revealed Mr. Straus's bearish essence and that is much more interesting than saying, "Mr. Straus was big and hairy."

Metaphors are also a powerful way to express emotions. Feelings are often tricky to describe. How do you explain sadness, excitement, fury? Metaphors can help.

For instance . . . meet Bertram Spanx. He's a great kid. Super smart. On the shy side. He's nice to his grandma, and he showers regularly. Bertram has a mad crush on Josie. She doesn't know Bertram exists. Or so he thinks until one day, in math class, Josie winks at him. No kidding. He didn't imagine it. How does Bertram feel? We could say Bertram is thrilled, but honestly, I think we can do better than that. How about this:

Bertram's blood carbonated on the spot. It bubbled and fizzled as it rushed through his body, tickling his veins, and finally settling in a sweet, frothy mess in his brain.

Fast-forward to the next day. Josie is winking at everyone. And her eye is looking bloodshot. The teacher sends her to the school nurse and asks if someone will accompany her. Bertram's hand shoots up. So does Lars, the good-looking star athlete. The teacher chooses Lars, the good-looking star athlete. Josie smiles.

How does Bertram feel now? He knows that the wink was not a symptom of her love for him, but just a symptom. He feels rejected. He feels sad. Oh, I think we can do better than that . . .

Bertram knew the truth. He was one of those houses that no one ever visits on Halloween. The house that gives out healthy snacks. The house that means well. The house that is no fun at all. Trick-or-treaters walk right by it and head to the fancy house next door, where they give out packs of Gummy Snails and GooGoo Puffs. Full sized.

Wait, but we can't leave Bertram feeling so rejected. Let's fast-forward two days. Josie has conjunctivitis.

That's right, pinkeye. She's not allowed back at school until it clears up, since pinkeye is nearly as contagious as the bubonic plague. Lars visited her once at her home, and he told everyone in math class that her eye looked all crusty and repulsive. Bertram wanted to punch him for that. Thankfully, he's the nonviolent type. Instead, he bought a package of baby carrots (good for the eyes) and a dozen purple tulips, and he went to visit Josie. She was really happy to see him, even though he had to remind her what his name was. They ate the baby carrots and watched soap operas, and before he left, Josie said, "Can you come back after school tomorrow?"

Bertram was so happy. So so so happy. Soooo happy. All right, maybe we'd better use a metaphor here. How about we use an extended metaphor? That's a metaphor that is repeated often or throughout a story. Here goes:

Finally, someone had finally knocked on the door of that lonely little house on Halloween. Someone whose eyes were crusty but beautiful. Someone who no longer wanted silly, sugary things but instead wanted something more substantial. The door opened and the light from inside that little house shone on the girl and the street and seemed to stretch all the way up to the autumn sky, illuminating the stars.

What happens after that? Well, I think that Bertram comes down with pinkeye. Josie brings him baby carrots, and they spend the afternoon reading poetry to each other. . . and everyone knows that poetry is filled with metaphors!

Next time you are trying to figure out how to describe something, try shape-shifting that thing with a metaphor. You never know when a cat's paw is a snowflake, when an old man is an unmatched sock, or when loneliness is a coral reef.

I DARE YOU
Write a metaphor for any or all of the following:
- The smell of your own skin.
- The feeling of waking up after a terrifying nightmare.
- A splatter of black paint on a white wall.
- The feeling of jumping a horse over a fence.

Smirking Similes
by Ellen

Simile. The word always makes me think of smile, but similes are more smirky than smiley. Unlike the poof! presto-change-o action of a metaphor, similes have a more wry, smarty-pants feel.

The official rule about similes is that they compare one thing with another thing, using the word "like" or "as", like these.

She was like a mermaid: Adorable on the surface, but a little fishy deep down.

OR

He was as nervous as a snowman in March.

OR

Pinkeye feels like having your eyeball marinated in pickle juice.

Smirk, smirk. See what I mean? Of course not all similes are the smarty-pants type, but when I read a simile, I can often picture the writer sitting at his or her desk, biting a thumbnail, and thinking hard about how to compare one thing to another thing in a new and interesting way. Here's another simile.

The tiny elves slipped through the open window like rainwater.

Can't you just see me tapping my finger against my forehead, thinking, "Elves slipping through windows . . . hmmm. Slipping like slippers (that's dumb) . . . slipping like honey (more sticky than slippy) . . . like rainwater. Yes!"

Tips for Developing Great Metaphors and Similes

1. Focus on the thing you are trying to describe. If it's an object or a living thing, imagine that it is right in front of you. Get a good look at it 360 degrees around (in your mind, of course). Concentrate intensely on the object for a while. Then relax and meditate. I don't mean that in a guru, incense-burning way. Just let your mind wander freely. Every so often let it wander back to the object, take a peek, then wander away again. After a while, you might find that an image pops into your mind. Or several images. Sometimes they don't really pop, but slowly develop, like a Polaroid picture (there's a simile!).

2. If it's a feeling you are trying to describe, try to remember a time when you experienced it yourself. Step into the feeling now. Pay attention to where you feel it in your body—your belly, your spine, your throat, the muscles in your face? Focus on it for some time, then let it go and follow the meditation technique above.

3. You may not trust your own mind at first. You may think the images that appear are totally random. "What on earth do my character's feelings toward her long-dead mother have to do with a snow

globe?" you might ask yourself. Give your mind the benefit of the doubt and consider the possibilities. Maybe your character only remembers the romanticized unnatural version of her mother—like a pretty figurine encased in a snow globe. Before you dismiss an image, check and see if some part of it connects with what you are trying to describe. You might be surprised at how ingenious you are!

I DARE YOU Write a metaphor or simile for the following:
1. Annabella's parents have just told her they are getting a divorce. How does she feel?
2. Principal Sykes, who is six-foot-three and walks with a limp, enters the classroom.

Ta-Da!

The End

by Ellen

Think about your story as a window in a house. You have drawn open the window's curtains so that your readers can watch your characters do things. You try and stay out of the way as much as possible (see "To Plot or Not to Plot," in Section 7 on page 46), allowing the characters to follow their desires without you interfering too much. However, it is up to you to decide when to close those curtains—in other words, when to end the story. Do you want to end it with a neat-and-tidy ending, or does a more complicated but less tidy ending appeal to you more?

Here are several types of endings.

1. Neat-and-tidy endings in which the main character's heart's desire has been achieved. These sorts of endings are generally "happy endings." It's a fairly satisfying, case-is-closed approach.

   Even in these happy endings, though, the character may have to sacrifice something or suffer some sort of loss to attain his or her desire. This makes for a bittersweet ending, which can be wonderfully powerful.

2. Endings in which the main character doesn't get what he or she wants, but the person does get what he or she needs. These endings are more complicated than neat-and-tidy endings and can be quite interesting. For instance, it may turn out that although the character's heart's desire was to win the national wrestling championship, what he really needed was his father's respect. Maybe he didn't win the championship, but through the process of trying to win the championship, he did realize that his father respected him all along.

3. Endings in which the main character doesn't get what he or she wants or needs. These endings

often have a slice-of-real-life feel to them. Things aren't neatly resolved. Problems still exist, yet life goes on. Yes, this type of ending may be sort of a downer, but life can feel that way at times.

4. There are also surprise endings, and any of the three preceding endings can have a surprise in it. Surprise endings are lots of fun, but you have to be careful that your surprise makes sense for the story and that you aren't just using it for the shock value.

The ending is also a point when the author's perspective can really shine through. Think about what has happened in the story. Think about the changes that your characters have gone through, what they may have learned (or not learned) along the way. You don't necessarily have to come right out and say what has happened, as in "Though Kara was much happier being a high school geek than a teenage pirate, she never forgot her days of pillaging and swashbuckling." Instead, you can suggest it. At the end of the story, you can zero in on Kara's bedroom closet, for instance, and show her pirate sword way back in the corner, behind the algebra trophy from math camp. Or you can show Kara jotting down the final answer on her biology test and, forgetting herself for a moment, she raises a fist and shouts, "Huzzah!"

Another technique is to show your character in a situation that she has experienced earlier in the book and reacting to it in a new way. I did this with my book *Pish Posh*. My main character Clara starts out as a huge snob who has no patience for sentimental things. By the end of the book, she has changed quite a bit. She's been humbled. She's no longer hard and cold. I wanted to show this in a powerful way, and I struggled with different possible endings. They all seemed too preachy. I wanted to demonstrate how she had changed rather than explain it. So I took a walk through the woods with my two large dogs and thought about everything that had happened to Clara in the story. I remembered a minor incident in which Dr. Piff, a very kind family friend, told Clara that he taps his foot three times on the ground when he enters Washington Square Park. The park had once been used as a graveyard for poor people. Dr. Piff says that he does this to say hello to all the old New Yorkers buried beneath the park. Clara scoffs at this idea as sentimental nonsense. And so I thought, what if I put Clara back in Washington Square Park at the end of the book, and I have her tap her foot three times? I liked the idea, so I tried it and it worked. I was able to show the readers that Clara had changed without having to explain it to them.

When you are trying to write the end of your story and feel stuck, try this:

1. Have a peek at the first sentence in your story. See if you can find clues for an ending in that opening. Does your ending have a connection with your beginning?

2. Take a walk. There is something magical about walking and thinking. It oils up the gears in your brain. While you're walking, think about all the things that have happened to your characters, about what they may have learned from their

experiences, how they have changed or how cir-
cumstances around them have changed. Gather
up everything you know about them. If you feel
overloaded or frustrated, just stop thinking about
it. Look around you and enjoy the scenery. Nice
and easy. Don't force it. When you get back home,
jot down your thoughts immediately. See if they
lead you to the right ending for your story.

Avoiding the Mad Dash
by Ellen

It's sometimes tempting to end your story too quickly.
Maybe you're bored of working on it, or you're nervous
about how you should end it, or maybe you have a deadline looming, so you make a mad dash for the finish line.

Mad-dash endings are generally not a great idea.
They feel rushed. They're usually pretty unsatisfying.
Your reader will know that you were making a mad dash
and be annoyed with you. You don't want your readers
to be annoyed with you. The next time you want them
to read one of your stories, they might say, "Mmm, you
know what? I have to go and churn butter now. Yep, I
churn my own butter. Takes forever. No time to read."

Or maybe they won't even be that polite.

Whenever you feel tempted to make a mad dash for the end, try these things:

1. Put the story aside. Do something else. Maybe churn some butter.

2. Reread your story from the beginning. This can be very eye opening. You may spot things in your story you hadn't noticed before, and this may give you fresh ideas as to how the story might end.

3. Go back to the technique described in "Stalking the Wild Character" (in Section 7 on page 48) of asking your characters what they want now. A lot has probably happened to them since the beginning of the story. Check if their heart's desire has actually changed. If it has, this may be a clue to how you want the story to end.

4. If you have a due date that is right around the corner, you can try to ask for more time. If that's not an option, chalk it up to a live-and-learn situation. Professional writers have to deal with deadlines all the time, so it's a good idea to get friendly with them now.

Next time you have a deadline, try and pace yourself. I find that writing fiction always takes longer than I think it will. You need time to think, to take your story in the wrong direction, to backtrack and take it in the right direction, to get writer's block, to think some more. And in between writing you have a life, full of homework and athletic events and hanging out with friends. However much time you think you need to write a story, double it and you'll come closer to the truth.

The End . . . Hey, Weren't You Listening? I Said The End!

by Ellen

There have been times when my story ended and I didn't know it. I just kept on writing and writing until I got that strange squirmy feeling that something wasn't right. (You know when you are talking on the phone to your friend and suddenly you realize that he or she is no longer on the other end and you've been chatting to yourself for the past three minutes? It feels something like that.) When I stopped and reread what I wrote, I realized that my ending was actually several pages back.

This happens more often than you would think. If you find yourself floundering around, searching for an ending, check and see if you might already have written the end. It might not have been what you had envisioned, so you simply didn't notice it.

Endings are tricky things. You don't always know where your story should end, so you just keep writing and writing and searching for the perfect way to wrap things up but nothing seems quite right, and . . . uh-oh. I think I just wrote past the ending of this section. Yeah, I think this section ended in the last paragraph. Okay, I'll stop writing now. Sorry.

Loose Ends

by Ellen

When you do come to the end of your story, check for loose ends. Loose ends are unresolved issues in the main plot or subplot. Have you left any minor characters dangling in the middle of a dilemma? Is there anything in the story that is going to make your reader think, Hey, wait a minute! What about [fill in the blank]? Loose ends can feel very unsatisfying to a reader, and can make them wonder if the writer simply wasn't paying enough attention.

Now, I'm not saying that you can't ever have loose ends. Life has loose ends, after all. However, try and make sure that you haven't left loose ends because

1. You didn't notice them.
2. You did notice them, but you didn't feel like dealing with them. (Like when aliens took over the school and levitated the gym teacher fifty feet above the soccer field. Well, now that the aliens

have been successfully vaporized by the sixth-grade Chemistry Club, you'll need to remember to somehow get that gym teacher down from the sky.)

The End? Really?
by Ellen

Finally, how do you know when you have the right ending?

Like so many things in fiction writing, it's a gut feeling, and it's hard to describe. But since this is a book about how to write, I'd guess I'd better try to describe it.

You might have the right ending if you:

1. Smile when you read the last sentence.
2. Cry when you read the last sentence.
3. Feel like you have nothing more to say.
4. Hear applause in your head (okay, that's only happened once to me, but it was very enjoyable).

section

18

Revision

The View from the Boulder

by Ellen

Writing your first draft is like taking a long, meandering hike through unfamiliar countryside. You don't quite know where you're going. You pass through crummy little towns that turn out to be captivating, walk down promising roads only to discover that they're dead ends. You keep taking wrong turns and have to backtrack and start all over again.

At the end of the hike (or sometimes when you are only partway through), you perch yourself on a huge boulder. From that height, you can look down at all the places you have been and can see where you got lost and where you found your way again. The view from the boulder gives you perspective.

When you are ready to revise your story, you are sitting on that boulder.

You need to have the view from the boulder to really see what your story looks like and to figure out how to make it better. Trust me, you can make your story better. All writers revise their work, often many, many times. It's nearly impossible to get a story just right with the first draft. I revised this section on revision four times!

Here are a few reasons new writers (and not-so-new ones) often feel squeamish about revising:

"I'll see all the things that are wrong with my story!" You will but that's okay. You have the view from the boulder now and can see your story much more clearly. When you understand what went wrong, fixing things is not such a scary process.

You'll also be amazed at how much you got right. Don't be surprised if you find yourself thinking, Hey, that was some pretty slick dialogue or that description of the twin-engine plane crash in the African bush was kind of ... well ... dare I say, genius!

"Writing the story was the fun part. Revising is sooo boring." Hardly. I'm not saying it isn't frustrating or difficult. It can be. But boring? Nope. Revising is like doing an elaborate, interactive puzzle. You rearrange some pieces. You toss some away and add new ones that you create on the spot. You try out different endings and see where they take you. It's actually fairly entertaining.

While you're having a cut-and-paste party, though, try and save all your drafts so that if you wind up wanting to use an earlier version of something that you changed (as I often do), it's not lost forever. That will just make you cry.

"My story is perfect just the way it is." It's not. Sorry if that sounds rude, but chances are pretty slim that your story is without a single flaw. This business of creating universes out of thin air is pretty tricky. A lot can go wrong. Personally, I can revise a book dozens of times and still find things that need improving. That's why I almost never reread my books after they're published. I always find things that I wish I had caught and changed when I was revising.

"I just like to write the stories for myself. I don't care if they're perfect." Fair enough. People like to write for different reasons, and some people don't care if no one else ever reads their story. If you're one of those kinds of writers, you may decide to skip the whole revision thing and no harm done. However, if you're the kind of writer who wants to have readers (as most of us are), you should probably have a second, third, and fourth look at your story to make sure it's read-worthy.

Here are some things to think about when you are revising:

Are there any obvious holes in the story? Is there anything that happens that makes no sense?

Are my characters' motives genuine? Is it clear why they are doing what they're doing, and saying what they're saying?

Have I made my characters' hearts' desire strong enough so that my readers will give a hoot whether they get it or not.

Can I sharpen up my character's dialogue so that it sounds more natural and authentic?

Are there any loose ends that need tying up or cutting?

Are there any points in the story that are boring? If so, can I either find the thing about it that is interesting and strengthen it, or delete it altogether?

Do any of the sentences sound clunky? Are my metaphors and similes so fresh that my readers will read them and think, Ooo, I never thought of it like that before.

Make sure that your spelling and grammar are correct. I know that's not terribly exciting, but it really is important. Bad spelling and grammar signal that you're just too busy to bother or you don't really care about your story. The mistakes might be so distracting that your readers will stop reading out of pure frustration.

If you are feeling especially overwhelmed by the whole revision thing, try this little trick that both Anne and I use all the time: Make the easiest changes first and save the really hard ones for last. You'll build your confidence with the easy revisions and get so involved with the whole process that by the time you reach the tough stuff, you'll be able to tackle it, no problem.

Finally, I'll tell you a true story. Last summer my horse Mischa got into some nasty burdocks. Not only that, he had been rolling around in mud, and I had neglected his grooming for far too long. When I finally took him in the barn to be groomed, his long white mane was in sad shape. His mane is thick and kinky to begin with, and the burrs and the mud rolling and whatnot had turned it into a mess of knots with lumps of burdocks woven into the hairs.

I was on the brink of giving the poor thing a crew cut when my teenaged neighbor and friend, Jessica, happened to drop by. She offered to help me groom Mischa, and I gratefully accepted. For an hour, Jessica patiently pulled out the burrs and untwisted, detangled, and unknotted

Mischa's mane. Unlike me, her face was not red and glowering while she worked. In fact, she looked perfectly content.

"Don't you find this frustrating?" I asked her as I tried to dislodge yet another burr from a tight bird's nest of tangled mane.

She thought for a moment. She's the kind of person who always thinks before she answers. "At first. But now I'm kind of into it," she said. Then she scratched Mischa's neck and told him, "You are going to look so beautiful when we're done."

I think that's how writers should approach revision. Get into it. Go slowly and patiently, and remind yourself how beautiful your story is going to look after you have worked out all the knots and tangles and burrs.

And unlike Mischa, your story won't roll around in the mud five minutes after you've finished with it.

I DARE YOU Dig through your old notebooks or computer files and find a story that you abandoned because it was frustrating you. Reread it. Revise it. See what happens.

Do All Writers Really Revise Their Work?

by Anne

When people talk about writing, they often focus on revision. But do all writers really revise their work? Yes, all professional writers revise their work. As well as any writer who truly cares about writing.

But although revision is one of the most important things that any writer does, we don't necessarily revise all our work. We revise the parts we don't throw out.

We revise the parts that need revising.

We don't revise just for the sake of revising.

On a typical day, we professional writers don't wake up, eat a healthy breakfast of Crunchios, flex our typing muscles, and then skip to our home office for a satisfying session of revision.

No. We wake up, down a cup of coffee, stumble into our home office, and stare blearily at the screen. Then we begin to either write v-e-r-y s-l-o-w-l-y or reread what we wrote the day before.

As we reread, we automatically tinker with our text. We can't help ourselves; that's the way our brains are wired. We continually rewrite and rethink our work. If I switch the order of these three sentences, we think, and change her hair color to magenta, won't his losing the secret treasure map make more sense? We hardly notice what we're doing. We don't say to ourselves, "Hey, I'm revising. Woo-hoo!"

For a professional writer, it's all writing. It's all about making our writing as imaginative, well written, and gripping as possible.

So we write—and rewrite—and rewrite . . .

Revision can be a magic wand that transforms your work. Saying no to your own words takes courage. In order to do it, you have to separate yourself from your writing. You are not what you write. What you write isn't you. It's part of you, but not all of you. You and your writing are always in the process of changing.

For me, the art of writing is not only knowing what to put in, but what to take out. Get rid of what doesn't belong. My rule is "when in doubt, take it out." (But always save deleted material, in case you change your mind.) Then see if the piece works without it. You can usually feel the difference immediately. Your tired old paragraphs will perk up as if they had just received a massive injection of B vitamins. They will become strong, energetic, and alive. Your writing will shine.

Eliminate Your Writing Tics
by Anne

Do you know someone with a tic? Maybe you have one

yourself, like you can't stop snapping off the split ends on your hair. Or when you're nervous, your eyes blink rapidly, or you run your tongue over your teeth, again and again. A writing tic is a word or phrase you can't stop using. It slips into your work when you don't notice and appears whenever you're feeling unsure of yourself. It's something important to watch out for when you revise. When I first started writing, for example, I used the word *suddenly* in almost every sentence. As in the following:

"She *suddenly* remembered that she had forgotten to take out the garbage. But when she closed the bag, it *suddenly* ripped, spilling crumpled tissues and half-eaten cheese logs onto the floor. She groaned loudly. Then *suddenly* the door burst open."

Thank goodness, I've stopped using *suddenly*— except when I really need it. *Suddenly* is like a strong spice; you only want to sprinkle a little of it into your story.

But lately I've noticed a tendency to use *just* in just about every other sentence. No matter how many times I delete the word, I just keep using it over and over. I just don't know why just just crops up over and over in my writing. I just have to stop relying on it.

I'm always on the prowl for my worst writing tics. You'd be surprised at how often they creep in.

section

19

Journaling

The Story of You

by Ellen

Your journal is the story of how you feel, how you think, how you view the world. It is the story of all the funny things that happen to you as well as the things that make you cringe with embarrassment. It is the story of your daily dramas, your moments of happiness and of disappointment, your memories, your family, and your friends.

In other words, your journal is the story of "you," and you are fascinating. I guarantee it.

Keeping a journal is probably one of the most important things you can do if you want to become a writer. For one thing, it will keep you writing on a daily basis. I like to think of journaling as training for the big marathon. You wouldn't run a marathon without having trained for months before. If you did, you probably wouldn't get very far. And there might be some vomiting involved. It's the same with writing. In order to write a really strong story, you need to practice with smaller chunks (pun not intended) of writing.

In your journal you can write short descriptions of people you know, paying attention to the small details like

the way they nervously jiggle their legs when they're sitting in class. You can write down scraps of interesting dialogue you may have overheard in the lunchroom. You can try your hand at short dramatic scenes, imagined or real. Just mess around. That's what journals are for. When it comes time for you to write your story, you'll be warmed up and ready to go. And you probably won't even vomit.

Journals are also the place where you can explore your own feelings honestly. When I'm feeling particularly confused or angry or hurt, I go to my journal in order to sort things out. Sometimes I write poems about what I'm feeling or draw pictures or just babble on and on. Let it be messy. Let it make no sense. It doesn't matter. Just let it spill out, and your journal will catch it and keep it safe for you.

Journals are also a great resource for story ideas. I like to read over my journals periodically (I still have journals I wrote when I was a kid), and I'm always amazed at how many ideas I get from them. In fact, the name for my character *Olivia Kidney* came from a journal entry that I wrote ten years before writing Olivia Kidney. I was working as a receptionist in a publishing company. It was a deeply boring job. I liked to imagine that my boss spent the night thinking up ways to bore me to death. One day, he handed me a stack of about a hundred blank envelopes and a list of names.

"Put all these names and addresses on these envelopes," he said.

Ugh.

But I did it. And as I was doing it, I saw a name that interested me: Olivia Kidney. Right away I knew I would use it for a character some day, so I jotted it down in my journal. Ten years later I found myself writing a book about an unusual eleven-year-old girl. The character was clever and tough but vulnerable, and she was not very popular at school. I had nailed her personality, but I couldn't think up a name for her. I looked through my old journals as I often do when I'm stuck for names or ideas, and I came across that old journal entry. There it was! Olivia Kidney! The name was quirky and potentially embarrassing. I figured that a girl who was named Olivia Kidney had to be both unusual and thick-skinned to withstand the teasing of her classmates. It was perfect, and if I hadn't jotted it down in my journal all those years before, I never in a million years would have remembered it.

Here are some things you can do in your journal.

1. Describe in detail the person in your class who interests you the least.

2. Take out all the junk in your pocket (or backback) and let all the items have a conversation with each other. For example:

New Calculator:	*Stop bumping up against me! You're going to make my keys sticky.*
Piece of Old Chewed Gum:	*I was here first.*
New Calculator:	*What's she keeping you around for anyway? Is she waiting for you to fossilize?*
Piece of Old Chewed Gum:	*You calculators all think you're sooo clever. As a matter of fact, she is planning on chewing me again the second she gets her braces off.*
New Calculator:	*And that would be . . . let me do some calculations here . . . in 739 days. Yeah, you'll be roughly the consistency of a lug nut by then. Yum, that'll be good chewing!*

3. Write a poem about your feet.

4. Write about the time you were absolutely furious.

5. Draw as many eyes that will fit on a page.

6. Write about your earliest memory.

7. Write down your dreams.

8. Go to a public place, like a shopping mall or a park, and write down everything you hear (conversations, music, the hum of machinery, the sound of the wind in the trees).

9. Describe one of your bad/disgusting habits and why you enjoy it so much.

section

20

Two Heads Are Better Than One

Daring Duo

by Ellen

Do you have a friend who also loves to write? If you do, you both might consider becoming writing partners. I have had a writing partner while working on most of my books. Here's how it works.

You and your friend will both be working on your own individual projects. You each might be writing a story, a book, poems, or smaller, more random pieces.

Sit down with your friend and decide how much writing you can both commit to every day. Maybe you can do one page of writing a day, or half a page. If you are writing on a computer, it might be easier to decide how many words you will write each day (you can use your computer's Word Count tool to quickly tally it up). Now make a solemn oath to exchange your writing every day (or five days a week, or even two days a week; it's up to you). You can either e-mail the writing to each other or exchange it in person.

I strongly suggest that you do not critique each other's work or give any negative feedback. Remember, you are giving each other first drafts. As I said in Section 2,

"Making a Mess," YES first drafts are . . . ugly. Critiquing a first draft is like telling a baby who is first learning how to walk that he or she is doing it all wrong. You'll just make the baby cry. Babies need time to try again and again before they get it right. So do you.

You can tell each other what you like about each other's work, however. You can tell each other which parts really popped, or which characters intrigued you. Be positive. Writing takes a lot of courage, and it's easy to get discouraged. You need to cheer each other on.

To make things official, you can actually sign a Writing-Partner Contract. Here is one that you can use, or you can just make up one for yourself.

Writing Partner Contract

ON

_____,
(DATE)

_____
(NAME)

AND

_____
(NAME)

DO HEREBY DECLARE THAT WE WILL EXCHANGE

_____ PAGES/WORDS OF WRITING

_____ DAYS A WEEK WITHOUT FAIL.

*We also hereby declare that we think
the other one is brave, supremely
talented, and generally awesome.*

SIGNATURES:

_____

_____

Part III
The Writer's Brain

The Writing Process

The Three-Hundred-Pound Draft

by Anne

When I was a kid, writing was a matter of following the rules. In school we learned grammar and spelling, and that was it. No one seemed to care much for imagination or ideas. The words *creative process* never crossed our lips. I wrote a total of five stories in public school between kindergarten and twelfth grade.

But still I feel sorry for today's students. Poor kids! I think. They have to brainstorm, pre-write, outline, story map, draft, edit, revise, give and receive critiques, and sometimes even publish. With all these steps, rules, and procedures, how will they remember to have fun with their stories?

It seems to me as if they are lugging three-hundred-pound drafts on their backs.

Maybe you think you're learning what "a real writer does" when you follow the stages of the writing process. But "real writers" don't necessarily care about the writing process. All they care about is writing a good story.

Don't Let the Writing Process Scare You Off Writing

When I'm writing, I never think about the writing process. I never worry about whether I'm drafting, brainstorming, revising, or editing.

I just write. My goal is to express my ideas in the strongest way possible.

I often—but not always—like to plunge right into a story from the first line, as if I'm putting one foot in front of the other. Not everyone is like this. I know other writers who go through several drafts before they even feel as if they're writing.

Sometimes a story is written in one burst of inspiration. There are people who tap into that vein of creativity very easily. Some of us have it happen once or twice in a lifetime. Most of the time, though, we use hammers and tongs to bring our stories to life. We work slowly and painfully (but we like it, anyway—at least most of the time).

There are many different ways to approach writing a story. You can sit down and write it. Or you can outline, map your imaginary world in Fimo, make macramé figures of your main characters, or do a story sculpture in Jell-O. If it helps you with your story, go for it. But if it doesn't, skip it.

On the other hand, I adore brainstorming, especially with a partner. I love it when ideas leap from brain to brain, like some sort of crazy lightning. I delight in scrawling idea fragments on a scrap of paper. (They're unreadable to anyone but me. And sometimes to me, unless I copy them out immediately.)

I don't always ask for critiques—and never before I'm finished with a manuscript.

I may share my work with the world, with two or three trusted friends, or with the inside of my file cabinet.

And sometimes I break or change my own rules. I'm in charge. It's my writing process, thank you very much.

Excuse me but I have to go now. There's a package of Jell-O, some hot water, and my latest story idea waiting for me downstairs.

Creative Process

by Anne

The words *creative process* remind me of individually wrapped cheese slices. Nothing could be neater, blander, or more boring than little square cheese slices in their little square cellophane wrappers. Can you imagine anything less like creativity? The creative process is never a neat, orderly progression from idea to finished story.

I wish there was another term for this. I don't really have a good substitute. When I think of the way I write, I think of a cave and a flashlight. The cave is the idea that I want to explore. The flashlight is my interest in the idea.

The more interest, the more powerful the light.

If I don't care about my idea, my flashlight will have a dim, puny light. It will barely light up the two inches in front of my nose. I'll probably lose my way in the dark, or fall down a deep crevice.

But if I'm fascinated by my idea, the light will illuminate everything around it. It will show me the walls of the cave and the path ahead. As I move forward and explore, I might find a secret passageway, a skeleton or two, or an underground river.

Always write about what interests you. Or find a way to make it interesting. Otherwise you won't have the energy to concentrate. Concentration is the key. It is like

I DARE YOU Remember a time when you were really, really interested in something? Maybe you liked to draw cartoons, or do martial arts, or look at the sky through a telescope. You found yourself learning more and more about your activity. You might not have felt like you were making any effort at all. It was just so much fun.

Try to approach writing the same way. Find a subject that you can't wait to write about. Experiment with different styles, and when something clicks, pay attention. Listen to your inner voice. If it tells you to follow a particular path, check it out.

For once, do exactly what you want. How does it feel? What happened?

Okay, try it again. And again.

the flashlight shining into the cave. It allows you to think about your story and to visualize your characters and their world.

Instant Pudding?

by Anne

There is a lot of time wasting in writing. Make up your mind that this is the way it is and don't let it bother you. Writing doesn't always have a clear ending or beginning. There isn't any one way to do it. And you usually have to throw a lot of it out.

Writing a book is like jumping into a lake and hoping that you can swim. I'm always amazed that I don't drown in the middle of my story. No matter how many books I've written, there's always a moment where I wonder how in the world I'm going to get through this one.

Fortunately, no one can see you when you write. No one sees how many mistakes you make every day. No one sees you take off with a minor character, forget about your original story, and then, weeks later, return ashamed and empty-handed. No one sees the full-scale devastation of entire manuscripts zapped with a single stroke of the delete button. No one knows how often you fall into the perfection trap. You spend hours or even days polishing one or two pages that you later realize don't even fit into the story.

Writing isn't a straight, purposeful line. You don't walk from point A to point B. You may jump to point Z; realize you hate it; hurry to Q; spend a few hours there; and then zip back to J, N, and C, only to end up at point A again.

Sometimes there's no way to find what works other than to try a lot of things out. So you take a few wrong turns. So you have to throw out a dozen or more pages, or even an entire book. So what?

Writing isn't instant pudding. You don't add boiling water and stir. It's a mysterious process that can't be hurried.

section

22

Hellooooo?
Anybody Out There?

Who Are You Writing For?

by Anne

When you write a story, you set an imaginary stage and people it with characters. Then the play begins to unfold. You're the writer, the actor, the producer, and the director. But who is the audience?

Who are you writing for?

You might write for the shy kid at the back of the class who never says a word. You might write for your best friend who collects shoelaces, or your worst enemy who sneers at your grammar mistakes. You might write for someone you met in a dream or in a book. You might write for a grandparent who always listens to you, or your third-grade teacher who brought lizards to school every day.

You can write for anyone you choose. Including only you.

When you write, reserve a tiny corner of your brain for your audience. You are speaking to him/her/yourself/them. (Or it? Maybe your audience is a tree.) You aim your words at them like arrows. You imagine them reading what you've written, laughing at your jokes, and maybe even sniffing a bit at the sad parts.

Make no mistake, however: Writing for an audience doesn't mean losing touch with yourself. You are at the heart of your story. Without your thoughts, memories, feelings, dreams, and wishes, your story is lost. Remember, it's your story. You decide what goes in it. Writing for an audience means that you shape your writing to communicate clearly, sharply, and powerfully with your readers. But still, don't try and second-guess what will appeal to your readers . . . write what appeals to you.

When I write, there's always an audience—either one person or many—lurking in my brain. Sometimes they even speak to me. "Tell me about her sister who tripped over the Christmas presents." Or, "Can you cut out that part about the singing barber?" Or, "Why does that boy use weird slang from the sixties?"

Occasionally, I write for myself. A strange thing happens then. If I don't believe anyone is going to read my writing, my words go limp and slide off the page. I turn out page after page of dull, plodding prose. It's as if my brain has gone on strike.

I write to communicate. I need to visualize someone on the other end of the line. I love shaping my thoughts for my readers. It's like trying to put together the most interesting puzzle in the world.

Writing this book, I'm thinking about you. Are you listening? Good!

section
23

Keeping Your Readers Awake

Waking Up Your Reader

by Anne

Think of your reader as a sleepy, dull person with dark circles under his eyes. He has so many better things to do than read your book. Like catch up on his sleep. Or change out of the rumpled pajamas he's worn for a week. Or lie on the couch and twiddle his thumbs.

But for some reason, the cover of your book catches his eye. He opens the book to the first page and reads a couple of sentences. He stifles a yawn. By the next paragraph, his eyelids are drooping lower and lower. Finally, his head thunks onto the table. A loud snore issues from his open mouth.

Congratulations. If it was your secret wish to replace artificial sleeping aids with healthy, natural organic boredom (no side effects, ever), you've succeeded.

On the other hand, you might prefer it this way: The sleepy, dull person picks up your book. He reads the first two sentences and his eyes pop open. He straightens up in his chair, stuffs a handful of popcorn in his mouth but forgets to chew it, and wipes the salt from his fingers on his pajama top. Suddenly, he's turning the pages as fast as he can. Sleep? Forget about it. He's not putting your book down until he's read the last sentence.

That's the kind of book I like to read. And that's the kind of book I hope to write.

Of course, not every reader will respond to a book in the same way. It would be terrible if they did. No one wants a nation of reading robots.

So, how do you keep your readers' attention?

1. It starts with you. If I'm bored, my reader is going to be even more bored. No one wants to read pages of monotonous "blabbedy-blab." (See "Blabbedy-Blab" in Section 13 on page 110.)

As I work on a project, I check my writer's temperature from time to time. Am I having fun? Am I interested? Do I care about what I'm doing? Am I so absorbed in my story that I forget about everything around me?

Does your writing project make your eyes sparkle and your fingertips tingle? Do you feel excited or compelled or fascinated by it? If you love what you're doing, you've made one person happy. And that's already an accomplishment.

2. Respect your readers. Your readers are smart, perceptive, and sensitive people. If you tell a story that they've heard a thousand times before, or dash off something sloppy, they'll definitely notice. They know the difference between a crackling good story and a clunker.

Give your audience only your best effort. Put yourself into your work. Remember that you're writing to communicate. Tell them a story that they'll never forget.

3. Master the art of surprise. You need surprise in your stories, just as you do in life. Surprise keeps things fresh. Surprise reveals the unexpected aspects of life.

Allow your characters to develop in unexpected ways. Allow yourself to be surprised by them. Remember, though, that even if you surprise your reader, it must still make sense.

Let's say you're writing a story about a girl whose best friend is always on a diet. One day, she goes to visit her friend and her friend has, amazingly, lost fifty pounds overnight. Surprising? Yes. Does it make sense? Not much.

However, if a fairy godmother has popped up earlier in the story, or if the girl has recently

 uncorked a genie from a bottle, or if she's gone through a time warp, we begin to understand how she lost fifty pounds overnight. It will still be surprising, but now we believe it.

Writers Are Strange Creatures. Thank Heavens!

A Funny Thing Happened...

by Anne

When I was a kid, I was quiet and shy, but intense. Whenever something happened to me, I'd make it bigger. When I told the story, I made it funnier, more tragic, more infuriating, more dramatic than real life.

My mother had certain words that she used to describe me: *melodramatic, fastidious, exaggerator,*

how about you?

BY ANNE

What faults do you have that might serve you well as a writer? Are you a daydreamer? Do you dream up stories about people you see on the street? Are you a little impractical, maybe rebellious? Are you stubborn? An idealist? Do you listen to the voices in your head?

procrastinator. It was all part of a storytelling personality. And my mother improved my vocabulary every time she called me a name. Sometimes, though, it seemed that she wished that I would turn into a new, improved version of myself, one who was more down-to-earth, efficient, and easy-going.

And it wasn't only my mother! Some of my friends used to get annoyed with me too. Sometimes I would see things they couldn't believe. Sometimes I could see things beneath the surface. I remember noticing a girl at a party and realizing that she was trying to steal someone else's boyfriend. But I couldn't convince my friends. "No, she's not," they said. But a few days later, the two of them were a couple.

By the time I reached adulthood, I was pretty frustrated. I couldn't seem to get through to other people. What was I doing wrong? I was just being me.

Then I became a writer and something very strange happened.

I put that same self into my writing. The same thoughts, the same observations, the same feelings. Only now I received praise for them instead of criticism. Strangest of all, I was now getting through to a lot of people. Like, millions.

As a child, I had great difficulty communicating with others. But I developed a way of thinking that served me well as a writer. I sharpened my observation, strengthened my sense of story, and became more intuitive. My most annoying traits became my best writer's tools.

Every character trait you have is a double-edged sword. It depends on how you use it. Find a place where you can shine. What drives others crazy may be your secret muse.

The Paranoid Fly

by Anne

When I was in school, I frequently got creative writing assignments that I thought were B-O-R-I-N-G. So I'd figure out a way to make them fun for me. In eighth grade we had to write a story from the point of view of an animal. My classmates got busy writing about cuddly kittens, loyal dogs, and noble horses. I decided to write a story from the point of view of a housefly. My fly had a paranoid worldview. The poor thing kept running into swatters, flypaper, and bug spray. Everyone was out to get him.

I thought my story was a great success. (I had a blast writing it.) But the teacher thought that I was making fun of her assignment. She gave me a D minus. My friend Michelle stood up in class and protested this injustice. She said that I done the work and deserved a better grade. The teacher didn't change my grade, but for weeks afterward my friends slipped drawings of houseflies into my locker.

The teacher hated my story. She didn't like me very much either. Maybe she was my first hostile critic. In response, my writer's ego came roaring out of the closet. She doesn't know what she's talking about, it hissed. She missed the point. She's an idiot. Okay, maybe I went too far in calling her an idiot. But my attitude helped me hold my head high. It helped me to believe in my story and myself. An ego isn't always a bad thing. Although most people aren't hostile critics, writers do occasionally receive criticism that is unfair or personal. That can hurt. Even fair, reasonable, well-intentioned criticism can sting. Those are the times when a thick skin and a strong belief in yourself can come in handy. Or just a good sense of humor.

section

25

Writer's Block 9-1-1

Hitting the Wall

by Anne

Writer's block always sounds like a prison or gulag to me—
the place where writers are punished. Imagine gray con-
crete walls and barbed wire looming up in the middle of
lush, hilly meadows. There are dozens of writers sniveling in
their gray, blank cells, gnawing on pencils, ripping up paper,
and beating their heads against the walls in sheer frustration.
They don't get released until they can write again.

This is how most writers experience writer's block:
You're doing great, you're sailing along, the writing is

flowing . . . then, without warning, you hit a wall. You can't write another word, or maybe you're writing the same thing over and over. You're stuck and you can't seem to get past it. No matter what you do, it seems like you're getting nowhere. You're bored, frustrated, and angry. You feel disgusted by the whole project. It's hopeless. You'll never get anywhere . . .

If you are working on a piece of writing and can't go on, here are some things to think about. First, take a deep breath. Frustration is a normal part of the writing process. It happens to everyone, even the most skilled writers. I don't usually have long periods of writer's block, but I do get "mini-blocks." Sometimes I get stuck on a page or a chapter or an idea that doesn't work. Like everyone else, I get overwhelmed and discouraged. A day or two of writer's block isn't the worst thing in the world, but it sure feels like it while it's happening. Try not to panic! Try to remember that it won't last forever.

If your writer's block goes on for a while, it can help to change your way of looking at it. Being stuck can mean a lot of things. Maybe you're going in the wrong direction, and your unconscious mind has figured that out. Now it's refusing to go another step until you recognize what's happening.

Another reason for getting stuck is that new material is about to emerge. Lots of times I get stuck right before a breakthrough. It seems like I'm going nowhere, or even backward, but later I realize that my unconscious mind was working all the time.

You might also be stuck because you've been pushing yourself too hard, and you need to give yourself a break.

Whatever the cause, you're getting information. There's a reason you're stuck, and when you figure it out, you'll be closer to getting through it. You may need to rest, make a change in direction, or wait patiently.

This brings us to the tricky part: Do you keep writing through the rough patch, or do you take a break? How do you know when to push harder and when to lay off?

Take your writer's temperature. Are you able to continue writing, or are you so frustrated that you might burst into tears? Do you never want to write again? Then do something really fun. Forget about writing and sit in a garden. Read a book; listen to music. Play a game with some friends. Then, when you're calmer, go back to it.

Then again, if you walk away every time you get a little frustrated, you never develop writer's muscles. Some of my best writing has come when I felt like I was getting nowhere. If I didn't keep at it, I never would have discovered what I could do.

So keep pushing yourself—a little—beyond what you think you can do. Say, "I will work on my story for fifteen minutes every day, no matter what." Set a small goal that you know you can achieve. Be faithful to it. If you slip up, try again the next day.

Here are some ways to spring yourself from writer's block prison.

1. First, try something simple. If you're typing, write by hand. If you write by hand, type.

2. Switch your point of view. Write from the point of view of a different character. Find out what the other characters in your story have to say.

3. Change your perspective. If you're writing as "I," write instead as "he" or "she" or even "we," or "you."

4. One of my favorite techniques is something I call "spilling." It means I let anything spill onto the paper without editing or judging it. Sometimes, as I mentioned earlier in the book, I even half close my eyes while I do it.

5. Pretend someone else is writing the book. What would J. K. Rowling do? Or your favorite author? Bring that person in to narrate your story for a while.

6. Ask for help. This is one of my favorite techniques! Sometimes the act of picking up the telephone and dialing my editor's number is all I need. Call

a friend and tell her your writing problem. As you explain it, you might get an idea right then and there. Or maybe she'll have a great suggestion. Even if you don't use her ideas, she can set you off on a new path.

Your Mind Is an Overflowing Toilet

by Anne

Whereas most people think of writer's block as having no ideas, it can also occur when you have too many ideas. Every now and then I experience a day or two of the "overflowing toilet of the mind." It is downright scary.

Ideas rush out at a fearsome rate. At first, it's exciting.
Your brain feels lit up and brilliant. It's thrilling to have
so many ideas. You want to watch your brain churn them
out, one after another. But then you realize that you have
too many. You can't possibly get them all down. Even
worse, you can't seem to concentrate on writing at all.
That's when your mind becomes an overflowing toilet.
The water won't stop rising. It spills over the rim and
floods the room. And you feel more and more anxious, as
if you're about to get carried away.

If this happens to you, do the equivalent of turning
off the water main. Take a deep breath. Then do something to mop up the mental flood. Take a walk, swim a
few laps, bike around the neighborhood. Then start writing, preferably with a pen, rather than computer. Writing
by hand will slow things down.

Take a single idea or thought that's rushing through
your head and concentrate on it. Wrestling with a single
idea will also calm your mind.

If all else fails, distract yourself. Watch TV. Read a
book. Talk to a friend. Change your train of thought.

section

26

Your Writer's Identity

What's a Voice, Anyway?

by Anne

Do I really need to tell you? You know what "voice" is: It's that thing that comes out of your throat. I mean, duh . . .

Sorry about the sarcasm . . . but in a way, it's true. Your writer's voice is what comes out of you. It's your voice. Simple? Yes—and no.

Finding your writer's voice can be as natural as breathing, or as long and difficult as a lifetime quest. Your writer's voice might be one voice, or many voices, or a series of voices that you discover, one after another. It may emerge the first time you write, or it may show up and then disappear. Or you may not find it for years.

Your writer's voice may be quiet or thunderous, flowery or clipped, poetic or barebones, chatty or mysterious. It may be none of these things, some of these, or all of them.

How to Find Your Writer's Voice
by Anne

1. Don't look for it. A voice isn't something you pick up on the side of the road, or find in a sale under a bunch of lime-green bedroom slippers. You don't find it lying on your desk after logging in 4,852.7 hours of writing, and it doesn't appear in a text message from your best friend. It's already inside you, waiting to be recognized. Perhaps you don't want to see it.

   Sometimes a voice can be a little scary. Your voice may be, for example, an angry one—and you think anger is bad. Or it may be comic—and you want to write serious novels. Or you have a secret desire to write about intergalactic warfare, even though your parents want you to be an accountant. Or maybe you lack confidence in your writing ability. There are all kinds of reasons you might not be able to easily connect to a voice.

Don't be discouraged. Most writers find a voice only after many false starts and a lot of trial and error.

2. Don't twiddle your thumbs, while you wait for it. (Unless you're practicing for the American Thumb Twiddling championship.) You need to prepare the way. Experiment with your writing. Take risks. Be playful. Try on a variety of styles, genres, and points of view. Assume as many writer's identities as you wish, until you find the unique combination that fits you.

As you learn more about writing and yourself, a voice or voices will begin to emerge. Some of them may feel shaky at first. They may feel uncomfortable, like new shoes you haven't broken in yet. That's okay. It's all part of finding out who you are as a writer.

3. Make connections. Having a voice is about making connections: with yourself, with others, with the act of writing. The more connected your writing is, the stronger your voice(s) will be. Here are some questions to get you started.

*What would you say or do if you had complete
freedom?*

*What are your secrets? Are they embarrassing,
painful, or beautiful?*

Who or what is most important to you?

Who or what do you love the most?

Who or what angers you the most?

When do you have the most fun?

What kinds of stories do you like to read?

What kinds do you like to write?

What do you love about writing?

What do you hate or dislike about it?

Who do you write for?

(Note: There are no "right" or "wrong" answers
here. So don't worry!)

4. Once you find a writer's voice, don't hold on too
tight. Think of your voice(s) as fluid and alive.
Allow them to change and grow as you do. Sometimes you need to let go to find a truer voice.

Voice Lessons
by Anne

I used to fantasize about belting out jazz standards in
front of a piano. But the truth was, I couldn't even sing

"Twinkle, Twinkle, Little Star." I was afraid to open my mouth. So one day, I enrolled in voice lessons. My teacher gave me a cassette tape of practice exercises. I took them home to work on. I closed all the windows and doors, and then vocalized for the first time in my life. My daughter, who didn't know I was practicing, thought that there was a screeching cat loose in the house.

My teacher taught me to visualize my head as an acoustic chamber. I imagined a large cathedral-like room inside my head and then imagined the notes I sang bouncing off the walls. Strangely enough, this made all the difference. I began to make sounds that resembled actual musical notes. If I placed my voice properly, it had strength, clarity, and resonance.

I was thrilled to pass out of the screeching cat phase. But I never advanced much beyond that. Although once I did manage to carry a tune in front of a dozen people without fainting, throwing up, or sobbing hysterically.

Even though I didn't ever get good at singing, my teacher taught me a valuable lesson. If you know how and where to place your voice, even a screeching cat singer can make pleasing sounds.

A writer's voice isn't an object that you can possess. Although when I hear a writer speak of his or her voice, I always imagine a gold statue enshrined in a cupboard.

But a voice like that won't ever do you any good. You'd always be polishing it, shining it up, showing it from its best angle. You might, however, feel nervous about taking it out and using it. You'd be afraid it might get dented or chipped. You don't want a voice that you're afraid of taking out of its case. You want a voice that has a lot to say and isn't afraid to say it.

Knowing where to place your voice is essential. Use your mind as an acoustic chamber. Find where your writer's voice has strength, clarity, and resonance. When you hit all your "right" notes, you may experience a feeling of joy or a sense of purpose. That may be a clue that you've found something real.

section

27

Begging, Borrowing, and Stealing

Writers Are Magpies

by Anne

Magpies are birds that are attracted to shiny pieces of fabric and glittery threads. Writers are people who are attracted to revealing detail, half-remembered history, and glimpses of people on the bus. We weave our stories out of memory, imagination, and observation.

When we write, all the separate strands blend together into one story. We can easily lose track of what we're remembering, what we're making up, and what we're borrowing.

At the age of eight, I published a poem called "Do You Like to Ride on the Subway?" in a children's magazine. Years later, when I was a teenager, I found a book of poetry and discovered the first two lines of "my" poem there. It wasn't my intention to plagiarize. I genuinely thought I had written the poem. (The rest of it came from my imagination.) But how could I have taken someone else's words without knowing it?

I still wish that I had realized that those two lines didn't just "come" to me. But now I understand better how it happened. Our subconscious mind gathers up thoughts, images, sounds, emotions—and sometimes a line or two of poetry—and holds everything in a sort of vast underground warehouse. Imagine it as a place where you can find whatever you need—from the gleam of tinsel in the snow after the holidays, to the memory of stealing seventy-two cents out of your mother's purse, to how you felt when your cat got hit by a car—and where you can pick and choose as you wish. A bit here, a bit there; and suddenly your story comes to life. It's all part of the magpie nature of writing.

Be the Author of Your Own Story

by Anne

Are you or aren't you the author of your own story? How can you tell what's yours or someone else's, what's borrowed, what's new, what's copycat, or truly you?

This seems like such an obvious idea, I sometimes think when I'm working on something. I remember having this thought about the very first picture book that I wrote. Am I sure I haven't read it somewhere before?

Sometimes an idea seems familiar, as if you've always known it. Even if you think your idea is like someone else's, but you really want to write it, go ahead. Several things might happen.

1. You might be wrong. Your idea might be one of those "I wish I had thought of it first" ideas. It might be one of those that seems plucked from the air. If that's the case, a lot of people might soon want to imitate you!

2. You may initially begin with an idea that is a lot like someone else's. But during the writing, the story might change a great deal. You will end up with an original piece of work. (You won't know until you try.)

3. You may end up writing a story that's very much like someone else's work. If it is, don't pass it off as

yours. Think of it as a writing exercise and see if you learned something from it. Maybe you figured out how author X writes such realistic descriptions, or how he or she makes their characters so deliciously kooky. Take what you learned and apply it to your own original work.

Every good story has a structure, just like every person has a skeleton and blood and bones. All human beings are put together in the same way, yet we're all unique and individual. A good story is the same way. There are infinite possibilities for writing a piece that comes from you. Your story doesn't have to be a mindless clone. Write a story that no one else in the world could have written.

P.S. A few words about plagiarism. When you plagiarize, you deliberately take someone's characters, dialogue, and plot, and then change a few details to disguise things. But why would anyone do that when they have their own thoughts, ideas, and feelings to explore?

I DARE YOU Try this "springboard" exercise

with a group of friends. The more people you can gather together, the merrier.

1. Get your pens and paper ready.

2. Take a sentence, any sentence you like. It should be a juicy one. Or it could be the first one that catches your eye. Let's open one of my favorite childhood books, *The Wonderful Adventures of Nils*, by Selma Lagerlof, to a random page, and choose the first sentence we see: "The wild goose didn't avoid the fox, but flew very close to him." Could you write a story from that? I think I could. But if you don't like it, find one of your favorite books and grab a sentence.

   You can also take a theme or idea for a starting point. You might choose one like "French toast" or "secrets" or "the day I lost my mind."

3. Have everyone write a paragraph or two using the sentence starter or theme you've chosen.

4. When you're done, take turns reading what you've written out loud. You will be astonished at the uniqueness of each person's imagination. If you do this regularly with the same group, you will soon come to recognize each person's "writing fingerprint."

section

28

The Writing Habit

My Writing Habit

by Anne

Here's what my writing habit looks like.

1. Wake up, get dressed, eat breakfast with my husband, slosh coffee into favorite orange mug, and stumble into home office.

2. Turn on computer. Read advice columns (I love advice columns). Scan news. Tell myself sternly to get to work.

3. Read gossip about spoiled movie stars. Order myself to get to work. Read news story about parrot who saves his family from overeating instead.

4. Turn on Word program. Finally!
5. Reread what I've written the day before.
6. Rewrite where needed.
7. Begin new work.
8. Write until
   a) satisfied.
   b) finished.
   c) so frustrated I can't write another word!
9. Turn off computer. Take break of at least an hour.
10. Repeat steps 4 through 9 as often as necessary to finish writing project.

It took me many years to develop a writing habit. I started with an hour a day. At first, it was after work, and then, when I was the mother of small children, it was late at night when they were asleep. I was very strict and forced myself up the stairs to my computer every night. "No matter what," I muttered to myself. Some nights I sat in front of the computer with a headache or a fever, forcing myself to write gibberish until the hour was up. Sometimes I wrote the same few lines over and over. As you know by now, sometimes I would just stare at the screen in a stupor. And sometimes I would actually write.

It didn't matter if I had to delete it all the next day. I had fulfilled my goal of sitting down to write for an hour a day. No matter what.

I made the transition from writing one hour a day to writing two or three hours when my kids were in pre-school. Then, I had entire days when they were both in elementary school.

It took years to build, but now I'm a full-time writer. (Just for the record, I never write nonstop for six hours. I write in short sessions of two to three hours. If I don't take breaks, my brain starts to overheat.)

Today, after almost thirty years, my writing habit is so much a part of me that I couldn't lose it if I tried.

Your Writing Habit
by Anne

Like anything else, writing is practice. You have to build up to it, like an athlete. As you begin to write, remember this. Don't push yourself too hard past your limits. It will only result in frustration and failure. It's much better to slowly build your strength as a writer. Start where you're comfortable and expand.

If you want to write, set yourself up with a schedule and a goal. It can be very simple, or more difficult. It all depends on who you are, what you want, and what works for you.

Say you can only spare fifteen minutes a day. Maybe you think that isn't enough—but it's better than nothing!

If you stick to your goal and write almost every day, even for a short period of time, you're developing the habit of writing.

You may want to write only a few paragraphs a day. You may want to tackle a big project, like a novel, right away. You may want to write poems, short stories, articles, descriptions, or character sketches. You may want to simply jot down ideas. You might write for a set period of time until you have covered three pages in tiny, scribbled handwriting. You can create assignments for yourself—for example, any of the many found in this book—or let yourself roam free.

I've tried many different kinds of writing and learned that some of them are not for me. I've devoted years to projects that have gone nowhere. Sometimes I like to imagine a giant overflowing wastebasket in the sky. Inside it are all my rejected picture book ideas; as well as a first novel with *irresistible* in the title (it wasn't); and a bunch of sad, wilted beginnings that never found their middle or end. There are also discarded chapters, abandoned characters, drafts galore, and many boring or aimless paragraphs. You could drown in that wastebasket! If you compare the sheer amount of writing in it with what's on the published shelf, my wastebasket wins a hundred to one. Behind every successful book is a lot of ripped-up, crossed-off paper. It's all part of the writing process.

Be sure to give yourself lots of appreciation every time you sit down to write. It doesn't matter if you end up throwing it all out tomorrow. You're building writing muscles. You're gaining confidence in yourself as a writer. And besides, the day after tomorrow, you might have a breakthrough.

The Wobbly Skater: Setting Goals
by Anne

Funny thing about goals—if you set them for yourself, you're more likely to reach them. I learned this when I was writing series. I discovered that I could set a goal that I thought was extremely difficult—say, writing a one-hundred-page book in three months—and then meet it.

Setting goals is a powerful thing to do for yourself. Just make sure that (a) you really want to do it and (b) it works for you.

If I set a goal to become a professional ice-skater, I'd be doomed to failure. I might fantasize about it when I saw ice-skaters gliding smoothly around the rink to romantic music, but I'm terrified of ice. I like my feet to touch the ground at all times. Plus, I don't have a good sense of balance.

For me, a realistic goal would be to get the courage to put on ice skates and wobble around the rink, holding very tightly to someone's arm. If I did this, I think I'd feel quite proud of myself! Maybe even prouder than when I finished the first Abby book on time, because I am way more afraid of ice than I am of hard work on a book.

Setting myself a goal to finish a book in three months was realistic for me because I'd already written fourteen books by then. But if you've never written a book before, don't scare yourself off by trying to do the same thing. Build up to it slowly, like I did. When I began to write, I set myself the goal of writing something every evening. Sometimes my "something" wasn't very much. Other reasonable goals might be: Write a chapter a week, or write one page every night, or finish a short story this month. It could also be: Try to find a writing partner, write down three story ideas every night before I go to sleep, or show the book that's been hiding in my drawer to a teacher or friend.

Make your goals a little bit hard, but not absolutely impossible. You'll be amazed at what you can do.

Time, Space, and the Power of Place
by Anne

Given tools, a writer can write anywhere. I've written in every room in my house, in cars, on planes and buses (although not very well), in restaurants, in cafés, and on park benches. I've written outdoors and indoors, in silence and in noisy crowds. I've written while the walls of my house were being torn down and while rocking infants to sleep. I've even written in the dark! (Handy writer's tip: Don't do it. Impossible to read the next morning.)

But if you're really serious about writing, you need to carve out a special writing place for yourself.

How to Create a Writing Space
by Anne

1. Take yourself seriously as a writer. Give yourself time and space. This is the most important decision you can make as a writer.
2. Find a place to write. You should feel safe and quiet and able to think. Your writing place doesn't have to be fancy. It can be a comfortable chair in the corner of your room. It can be a seat at your desk, the edge of your bed, or the back stairs. It can be a table at a favorite café or library. Some

writers feel safe and quiet and able to think in the midst of noise and activity. They can concentrate in a school cafeteria or a bus station or in a gymnasium with blaring rock music.

3. Make it a place you love. If clutter distracts you, make sure everything has a place. If chaos stimulates your brain, let the mess pile up! If music helps your imagination, turn it on. If you like to gaze at photos or paintings, hang them on the wall. Surround yourself with your favorite objects:

rocks, old typewriters, books, slingshots, dolls, animal skeletons, anything you like.

Maybe you don't care where you work. That's okay too, as long as you have that space in your brain.

4. Use ritual and habit to create a writer's space. Go to the same place, at the same time every day, and see what happens. (When I sit down at my desk, I can't help writing! That's the power of habit.)

Have a ritual to start your writing time. In the old days, writers sharpened pencils, or put fresh sheets of paper into the typewriter. Many writers read before they write. Or they straighten their desk. (Kind of boring, but true.) I bring a cup of tea to my desk. That signals that I'm ready to start writing!

5. Then do it!

section

29

Belly Buttons

Are You an Innie or an Outie?

by Anne

When it comes to belly buttons, there are innies and outies. When it comes to writers, there are the more-is-betters and the less-is-mores.

More-is-better writers like to describe everything in the fullest, most flourishing detail. Their writing is expansive, talkative, descriptive, detailed, and illustrative. They are the people who write one-thousand-page tomes. Think *War and Peace* or *Harry Potter*.

Less-is-more writers like to keep it short and simple.

They need to crystallize their thoughts. The best example of less is more is Japanese haiku, where a moment—a universe—is contained in seventeen syllables.

Sometimes it seems like there's a conspiracy against plain, direct writing. Some teachers think "more is better;" they reward students for lots of adjectives and adverbs, or they require students to meet a word count or page requirement. Even if the students want to get to the point, every flowery adjective helps. Or perhaps they want to impress their friends with their super-sized vocabulary. (Guilty! I hate to admit it, but I peppered my early stories with words like *eleemosynary* and *conjecture*.)

Are you an innie or an outie? Do you like to get to the point, or do you like to explore every possible nook and cranny of your story? Do you write very simply, or do you express yourself in elaborate sentences? Or are you a hybrid combination of the two? Maybe you switch back and forth, depending on what kind of story you're working on.

Don't forget—just because you've discovered a strange, unaccountable fondness for sentences that go on for pages at a time doesn't mean you can't switch to short, declarative sentences any time you choose.

I DARE YOU Write a story as a less-is-more writer. Make your voice simple, clipped, and to the point. And then try writing the same story in a more expansive style.

Did changing your style change your story? Did it change the way you thought about your characters or what happened to them? Which style did you like best? Which felt more natural? Compare the stories. Which one was more powerful? Or did both stories have powerful moments? You might want to combine the best parts of each.

Accentuate the Positive

by Anne

There's a famous song by Johnny Mercer and Harold Arlen that goes: "Accentuate the positive / Eliminate the negative." Not only is this a good song, but it happens to be excellent writing advice.

It's good to know all the different parts of a story: plot, character, description, setting, dialogue. It's important to use them all in your writing. However, writing a story isn't like carving up a pie. You don't need to make each slice equal.

For example, there are writers who write gripping, page-turning plots, and others whose stories are very atmospheric. They make you feel like you're there. Some writers have an ear for dialogue, or a gift for language, whereas others develop complex, fascinating characters. Most writers mix up these skills, and a very few do it all beautifully.

Perhaps you feel that you can't be a writer if you haven't mastered all aspects of story writing. Not true! Be the writer you are, not the one you think you should be. Start where you are and expand your skills.

I used to be intimidated by plots. My first book was rejected for its lack of plot. In the early days, whenever I began a story, I panicked. "Oh no, I have to come up with a plot! I need to know what happens next: I need to figure out every turn and twist of the story. I have to have all the answers before I even start writing!" Then I'd go breathe into a paper bag for a while before I could sit upright at my computer again. But writing the Abby Hayes and Sister Magic series was like boot camp for poor plotters. I learned to think about my character and her heart's desire. And then I'd think about what kind of obstacles might keep her away from it and what kinds of things might help her achieve it. Plotting is kind of like a series of fortunate—or unfortunate—events. (Thanks for the term, Lemony Snicket!) But no matter what happens in the story, for me, it's all about the characters. Who they are, how they respond, the choices they make— that's what I love to think and write about.

My son, Max, on the other hand, loves dialogue. He has a gift for getting to the point with the fewest words possible. One or two of his teachers pushed him to write descriptive pieces in a more flowery style. But it just wasn't in his nature. Those writing assignments received poor grades. He didn't say much about them, but they made me mad.

In high school, he discovered a talent for playwriting. His plays were produced in his school, and he won some awards. He had found a place where his gift for dialogue and stripped-down writing became an asset, not a fault.

Play to your strengths, not your weaknesses. You don't have to perfect every aspect of writing. Concentrate on what you're good at, and especially on what you love. Then make it even better.

"Smart" Class, "Dumb" Class

by Anne

On my very first school visit as an author, I had an unforgettable experience. I made my presentation, and, when I was done, I asked if the students had any questions for me. Many kids raised their hands. I called on them one by one. I was thrilled when they asked dozens of perceptive, intelligent questions. We had a spirited, lively exchange. Then the class was over.

The kids went on to their next class, and, for a few moments, I was alone with the teachers. I began to praise the students and their wonderful questions.

"Did you hear what Marcus asked?" one teacher blurted. The boy she was talking about had asked a particularly interesting question about the images that went through my mind as I wrote. Twenty years later I still remember it.

"I can't believe it!" another teacher said.

A third teacher informed me that this was the "dumb" class.

"But they asked such brilliant questions," I said.

"Wait for the next class," she said. "They're the really good students."

Wow, I thought. The next class is going to be even more amazing.

I was also angry. The kids I had just spoken to were intelligent, thoughtful, and sensitive. They were the opposite of dumb. Why didn't the teachers see that?

The "smart" kids filed in. They seemed like nice kids. They listened quietly as I made my second presentation. When I was done, I again asked for questions. Not a single kid raised a hand.

"Ask me anything you want about writing or being a writer," I encouraged them. "There are only two questions I don't answer: how much money I make and how old I am."

The "smart" kids looked at me blankly. They didn't even smile. Then one girl dutifully raised her hand and asked me how long it took to write a book.

"It depends," I said, and explained how every book requires a different amount of time.

The class was over. I left the school.

For the next few days, I kept remembering the faces of the so-called dumb kids. I thought about their lively curiosity and responsiveness. I also wondered about the dullness of the "smart" kids. Were they too afraid to ask stupid questions? Had they lost the habit of curiosity?

I've never been able to forget that school visit. It taught me not to make assumptions about any group of students. It also taught me that smart can be dumb, and dumb can be smart.

People often judge one another in limiting ways. If other people don't believe in you, perhaps they are wrong. What others think are your weaknesses can often turn out to be your greatest strengths.

section

30

Criticism

Choose Your Readers Wisely

by Anne

It's great to get feedback. But like everything else, there's a time and place for it. Even a tree is small and tender at the beginning of its life. Have you ever walked down the street and seen tiny saplings protected by wire fences or cloth wraps? Do the same with your new, tender ideas. When you have a new idea, you need to protect it so it can grow.

Don't go around asking for feedback from lots of people. Someone might say something discouraging. And then you might abandon your idea before you've had a chance to explore it and decide for yourself whether it's a good one or not. I learned this the hard way. Once, when I shared an idea, one of my relatives said, "Oh, you can't do that." (How did she know?) Someone else said about another idea, "That's been done before." (Of course it had been done before! You can say that about almost anything.) If I had listened to them, I would have given up right then and there. Fortunately, I'm stubborn. I ended up writing—and publishing—both ideas. However, I blocked the negative feedback so thoroughly that I can't remember which books they were!

When you're starting out, get advice from one or two friends whom you trust. Once your story is written, then you can share it with more people. They may give you advice on how to improve it. That's great!

If you've completed a story, congratulate yourself. Work on it; make it better.

And then go on to the next idea.

Qualities of a Good Reader/Editor

by Anne

Here are the qualities of an ideal reader/editor.

1. Honesty. Doesn't tell you your writing is good if it isn't.

2. Sensitivity. Is considerate of your feelings. Tells you what works, as well as what doesn't.

3. Cares about what you are trying to do. Wants to help you do it.

4. Has respect for both you and your writing.

5. And, of course, has excellent judgment about writing!

How to Tell Good Criticism from Bad Criticism

by Anne

How do you tell if the criticism you're getting is good or bad? Ask yourself these questions:

1. Does it make your work stronger?

2. Does it respect the spirit of your writing?

3. Does the person offering it understand what you're trying to do?

4. Does the criticism help you understand why something doesn't work?

If you answered no to any of these questions, you might want to consider ignoring the criticism.

How to Take Criticism

by Anne

When someone critiques your writing, take a deep breath. Then try to remember the following points:

1. Keep an open mind.
2. The reader/editor is your friend. If the comments improve your work, it makes you look good.
3. You are not your writing. Your writing is only a small part of you. If someone criticizes it, he or she is not criticizing you.
4. Try to find something helpful, even in a negative critique.
5. If it doesn't help, ignore it.
6. Trust your gut.
7. Admire your own courage. It isn't always easy to ask for criticism, even for professional writers!
8. If more than three people make an identical criticism about your writing (e.g., "It has no plot"), it's probably true.

Reasons for Rejection

by Anne

Rejection is the universal writing experience. Every writer goes through it. Your teachers, friends, or family

might not like your story. Your father or sister might be shocked or angered at what you've written. ("What? You wrote a story about my snoring? And you read it in front of the entire school?") Your teacher may give you a failing grade if you don't do the assignment correctly. ("Aliens at a trailer park? During your summer vacation? I don't think so.") Your friends might not like what you've written. ("No, I'm not tired." Yawn. "Your story is okay." Yawn. "Can we watch TV now?")

If you're a professional writer, editors might reject your work, critics might make fun of it in print, or readers might refuse to buy it. (Or all three for a triple whammy!) Face it, if you don't bury your writing in a hole in the backyard, or burn it regularly, and if you're brave enough to show it to someone, sooner or later you're going to be rejected. Try not to take it personally. It happens to all of us. And rejection doesn't necessarily mean that your story stinks.

For example, you may have written a fine piece about aliens in a trailer park, but the teacher wanted you to write something more realistic. Or you embarrassed or hurt someone, so that person hates your story. (Remember, you'll want to change names and personal details to avoid this.) Or your friend loves gory, blood-drenched thrillers, and you've written a tender, lighthearted love story.

If one or two people don't like your story, don't worry. It could have nothing to do with what you've written.

section

31

A Writer's Life

Is This Your Idea of Fun?

by Anne

Is your idea of fun . . .

- sitting in a room by yourself all day?
- staring at blank pieces of paper while you cast about for ideas?
- writing and rewriting the same sentences over and over?

Yes? Well, have I got a career for you! To be a professional writer, you will need the following skills:

- Time wasting
- Daydreaming
- A knack for noticing things that annoy other people
- A delight in playing with words
- Stubbornness
- A slight touch of insanity

The Writing Life

by Anne

Nobody feels sorry for writers.

If we want to write in the middle of the night, in a tree house in the backyard, wearing an electric lime green and orange ball gown, a beanie cap, wool socks, and Elmo slippers, that's our business. No one tells us what to do, or how to do it.

It's a dream job, so we shouldn't even think of complaining.

Nevertheless, I'm going to complain. You should at least know what you're getting into.

1. Writing is some of the hardest work in the world. I call it "mental rock breaking."
2. Writing is lonely.
3. It takes a long time.

4. Even if you spend years on a project, you still might not succeed.

But . . .

I also don't want to lie to you. Writing is one of the world's greatest jobs. Let's talk about why.

1. You're in charge. You set your hours: all day, half a day, three hours four times a week, or on weekends only.
2. You choose your working space: tree house, basement, closet, café, or the biggest and best room in your house.
3. You choose your method: by hand, by typewriter, by computer, by dictation.

And, (this gets better) . . .

4. You're in charge.
5. You choose what to write: science fiction, fantasy, mystery, romance, historical fiction, nonfiction, technical writing, children's books, biography . . .
6. You choose the characters, the setting, the conflict, and the style. (Okay, maybe some of them choose you, but still . . . without you, they'd never breathe or speak or have a life.)
7. You choose whether to write in first person or third person. You choose whether his eyes are blue or gray. You choose whether she has a temper

or is just too sweet to be believed.

8. You can create a universe from the smallest seed of an idea.

9. Your words, written in a solitary room by a single person, have the power to touch millions. They might turn someone who hates reading into a book lover. They might change the course of someone's life. I once read a story about a famous

actor who spent his teens lying, stealing, and beating people up—until he read Shakespeare.

I'll tell you the truth. Here's the best part of being a writer:

*Your words can
change the world.*

Appendix

Spilling Secrets

Anne Asks Ellen

Anne: *How did you get started?*

Ellen: It started with horses. I loved horses. I grew up in New York City, where the only time you ever saw a horse was when it was pulling a carriage, or when a fancy person rode it through Central Park. I was not a fancy person. So instead of riding on them, I wrote about riding on them. It was almost as good as the real thing. Well, maybe it was even better because in my stories I was able to ride my horse through the Sahara and over high fences on the Olympic equestrian team and occasionally I dashed across the English moors on a high-spirited chestnut stallion.

Oh, and in real life, I am allergic to horses.

Anne: *When did you first realize that you wanted to become a writer?*

Ellen: It was a real ta-da! moment. I was in the school library looking for a book to read. The librarian suggested *Harriet the Spy* by Louise Fitzhugh. I found it on the shelf, pulled it down, and started reading the first few lines. It was so good that I sat down on the floor, stuck my nose in the book, and was instantly lost in Harriet's world. I don't remember what yanked me back into reality (probably the librarian telling me to get up off the floor), but I suddenly realized that the best books in the world were written for eleven-year-olds . . . which was great, because I was eleven. On the other hand, my twelfth birthday was right around the corner, and after that I'd be a teenager, and after that . . . holy cannoli, adulthood. Then what on earth would I read? I was horrified by the thought that I would get "adult amnesia" and forget about all the great kids' books. So I decided then and there that even if I couldn't always be eleven, I could always write books for people who were eleven.

Anne: *How long did it take you to become published?*

Ellen: It took a long time. No, actually it took a loooooong time (my first short story was published in a magazine about five years after I graduated college). But in the end, that wasn't such a bad thing, because it took a loooooong time for me to become a good writer. While I was getting rejection letters, I was still writing and reading lots of books and figuring out how to create a story that people would want to read.

By the way, you might think getting published is the greatest thrill ever. It is pretty great, don't get me wrong. But in my experience, finishing a book and knowing that it's good, is much more thrilling than getting published.

Anne: *What helped you the most when you began?*

Ellen: Weirdly enough, one of the things that helped me the most was a rejection from a teacher. I was in college and I wanted to become a creative writing major. I gave a bunch of my short stories to my writing teacher to see if she'd let me in the program. She wrote me back saying that I wasn't good enough yet to be in the program. Instead of getting discouraged, I got angry.

"Big mistake, lady!" I said to myself. "I'm going to hang on to your rejection note, and when my first book is published, I'm going to send you a copy of it along with your stupid little note." It would be the ultimate nah-nah-na-na-nah!

I put her note in a manila envelope. And then I got into the program without her. A different teacher let me in. For the next few years I wrote like mad. After I graduated, I churned out short stories and a novel for grown-ups and finally my first kids' book, *Olivia Kidney*. All that time, I kept that hurtful rejection note tucked away in my desk drawer, waiting for my big moment of revenge.

Finally my first book was published. I opened the drawer and pulled out the dusty manila envelope with the rejection note. It was then that I realized two things: (1) That teacher did me a favor by rejecting me. It made me rebellious. It made me want to fight to prove her wrong. (2) She was probably right not to let me in the program. I think my writing was pretty lousy back then. In the end I did send that teacher a copy of my book, but instead of including the rejection note, I included a Thank-you note.

Anne: *What was your biggest obstacle as a beginning writer?*

Ellen: I have two brothers who are impossibly smart, and as a kid I always felt like the dumb one in the family. How could I be a writer, I asked myself over and over, if I wasn't smart? Writers are witty, quick-with-a-comeback sort of people, I thought. I was always slow with getting my words out when I spoke, and the words I did manage to get out were not what you would call clever. But the thing was, every time I had almost convinced myself to forget about becoming a writer, I would read a wonderful book and think, Oooo, I want to write something as great as this! Then I would snatch up my pen and launch into writing a new story.

I still struggle with not feeling smart enough. I bet lots of other writers do too. When I'm feeling particularly dumb, I go back and read things that I've already written. "There," I tell myself, "you were able to write that story, weren't you? And that story was pretty good, which means you can't be a total dope." That often helps. And anyway, the only other option is to never write again.

And that's really not an option.

Anne: *Tell me about your family.*

Ellen: When I grew up, books were a big part of our family life. Our parents read to us a lot when we were little, and even when we were older (I still love being read to!). One of my favorite memories is that whenever I was home sick with a cold, my mother would read *Mary Poppins* to me. On some Saturdays, our parents took us to a used book shop on Manhattan's Lower East Side. It was one of those ancient stores with creaky wooden floors and the moldy smell of old paperbacks everywhere. Our parents set us loose, and we rampaged through the place, meeting my parents back at the checkout table with armfuls of books that sold for a dime a piece. I just loved that!

My parents were very supportive of my decision to be a writer. For many years after I graduated college, I waited tables at night and wrote during the day. Even though I hadn't earned a single penny from my writing, my parents never said, "Oh, come on, Ellen. Why don't you just give up writing and get a real job." They insisted that if I kept at it, I'd get published some day. They encouraged me to take the chance on pursuing what I loved to do. Young writers need a couple of cheerleaders at their back.

Actually, they need an entire squad.

Anne: *Who are your literary heroines and heroes?*

Ellen: I love Willy Wonka because he is totally mad and deeply good. I love Luna Lovegood in the Harry Potter books . . . again, totally bonkers but with a heart of gold. Then there's Claudia in *From the Mixed-Up Files of Mrs. Basil E. Frankweiler* because she really understood that great adventures take guts and plenty of sensible planning. I adore Uncle Vartan from your Sister Magic series because he is a grown-up who never grew up—the best kind of grown-up as far as grown-ups go—and he can do magic to boot.

Anne: *What or who inspires you?*

Ellen: Books often inspire me more than anything. I'll read something really great and think,

Oh, I want to make other people sink into a book like I just did!

Anne: *What were your favorite books when you were a kid?*

Ellen: I loved *A Wrinkle in Time*, *Harriet the Spy*, *Charlie and the Chocolate Factory*, *The Changeling*, *From the Mixed-Up Files of Mrs. Basil E. Frankweiler*, *Freaky Friday*, *The Secret Garden*, and so many others.

Anne: *What do you love/hate the most about writing?*

Ellen: Things I love about writing:

Getting up in the morning and stepping into a world that doesn't exist.

Finding out about things I'd never known because I have to research them for a book, like how to do an ollie on a skateboard or how to build a radio telescope or where to find a secret passageway in a Scottish castle.

Creating interesting characters, then getting to spend the day with them.

Receiving letters from kids who have read my books and have been changed—just a little—because they did.

Things I hate about writing:

I guess I don't really hate anything about writing, but there are lots of times when I slam my head down on my desk and moan, "This is hard!"

Then I have a strawberry Twizzler and feel a little better.

Ellen Asks Anne

Ellen: *What was it like growing up in a writing family?*

Anne: Growing up in a family of writers, you might say I spooned up the writing atmosphere with my breakfast cereal. It all began when I was five years old and my parents decided to become writers. It had taken them a lifetime to arrive at this decision, but for me, life changed overnight. Suddenly my family—which up until then had included me, my brother, and newborn baby sister—turned into a nonstop, 24/7 writers' boot camp. Every morning I awoke to the clicking, ringing sound of two massive electric typewriters. Half asleep, still dreaming a little, my head on the pillow, I knew that all was well in the world when I heard the keys of my parents' typewriters clattering loudly. That was the opening music to my day. Later, there was another, less enjoyable writing ritual to be endured. When my baby sister took her nap, my mother locked my brother and me out of the house so we could "get some fresh air." Bored and cold, we banged on the door and whined to be let in. My mother was adamant; we needed fresh air to be healthy. Translation: She needed writing time.

There were riches here for a future writer. We had a house filled with books, there were constant discussions about writing, and I had the riveting example of my parents making their writing dream come true. My courage to be a writer came from watching them when I was young. I saw how hard they worked, the time it took, and the discipline they needed. All of this was tremendously helpful to me later in my life.

Ellen: *How do you know when a book is done?*
Anne: When I can't go any further.
When it "feels" done.
When I stick a knife into it and when no crumbs cling to the blade.
When I refuse to write another word.
When the story lies down and refuses to budge another inch.

P.S. I don't always know when it's done. But usually I figure it out, sooner or later.

Ellen: *Did you always want to be a writer?*
Anne: Here are all the things I wanted to do when I grew up.

Artist. I really wanted to be an artist. I went to art school, and then I dropped out after a year. My younger sister, Maia, who was talented in all the arts, including writing and music, was the one who became a serious painter.

Children's book illustrator. I adored children's books and their illustrations. I was always drawing—and writing, although I didn't pay much attention to that.

Nuclear physicist. Seriously. When I was in seventh and eighth grade, I attended a program at Syracuse University called Science for Young Scientists. Your teacher had to nominate you for attendance, so it was a real honor. Each Saturday morning, S.U. science professors would give lectures on subjects like "how we would write a universal language to communicate with other life forms in the universe," or "how do light waves work?" or "the structure of an atom." The professors were incredibly creative and interesting in the way they presented their topics, and they sparked a desire in me to delve into science. Unfortunately, I didn't get any encouragement outside of the Saturday morning lectures, and I soon lost interest. But I always think of those lectures as one of the best educational experiences of my life.

Ballerina. Ha! I was not what you call terribly coordinated. I didn't even like ballet. I just liked the thought of myself as a beautiful, graceful, gliding ballerina. Seriously, I was one of the gawkiest pre-teens around.

I didn't want to be a writer. Not until my teens. And then it was just a whisper in my mind. I "forgot" about it, mostly, for another ten years. I did a lot of other things, like go to school and work as a bank teller, an au pair, a housecleaner, a factory worker, a secretary, a receptionist, an administrative assistant . . .

It was while I was an administrative assistant that I had my "aha!" moment. My boss had asked me to research air conditioners and to write up a report comparing different models. As I summed up the information, I found myself rewriting and polishing each sentence. Then I had an epiphany. No one in this office cares whether the writing flows, except me, I realized. My boss wants hard facts. I want good writing. In spite of this realization, I couldn't stop myself from tinkering with the words. I suddenly understood that this was what I

most cared about. From then on, I knew I
was a writer at heart.

Ellen: *Give us some advice for young writers.*

Anne: 1. READ, READ, READ.

2. Be a sponge. Soak up everything you
   can. Learn about the world. Learn
   about yourself.

3. Stay alert. Keep your eyes open, your
   mind sharp, and watch what your senses
   tell you.

4. Keep an open mind.

5. Try to understand other people's point
   of view. (I admit this isn't always easy or
   simple. But it's very powerful.)

6. Listen to others, to your own secret
   voice, to nothing at all.

7. Write regularly.

8. Do lots of things other than writing.

9. Do things that you wouldn't ordinar-
   ily do, that might even scare you a little.
   Stand on your head. Sing in front of an
   audience. Learn to play chess. You get
   the idea.

10. Have fun. Be playful.

Ellen: *What was your biggest obstacle when you began writing?*

Anne: Mood swings. One day I thought I was brilliant; the next day I was a complete, utter idiot. My mood swings almost immobilized me. I felt terrified to write. What saved me was the determination to keep on going, no matter what. By sheer willpower, I managed to complete one book, then another. And then I wrote another and another. In the course of writing these first books, I discovered that sometimes I felt like an idiot and wrote well. Sometimes I felt like a genius and wrote trash. Or the opposite might be true. When I realized that my moods had nothing to do with my writing, I started to pay less attention to them. Now mood swings no longer rule me. Sure, I have good and bad days like everyone else. But they don't throw me off course anymore. I know they are part of every writer's inner landscape.

Ellen: *Where are your favorite place(s) to write?*

Anne: I can write almost anywhere. And I have! But I like sitting at a desk with a view out the window. If possible, I also like lots of light, water, and trees. I prefer an orderly, spacious room with lots of books on the shelves and paintings on the walls.

Right now, however, my office is covered with papers, piles of old manuscripts, and bills to pay. But I'm writing, anyway. And I hope to clean it up soon!

Ellen: *Do you ever feel like giving it up altogether? If yes, what keeps you going?*

Anne: Yes, sometimes I get really discouraged.

But I can never think of any other job that I would enjoy as much, or that would give me as much satisfaction and pride, or as much control over my daily life.

I can never think of any other job where I can "talk" to millions of kids, or where I can shape the raw material of my life into imaginative stories.

Ellen: *Favorite books as a kid?*

Anne: You are opening a Pandora's box (of books) here.

Earliest Book Experience

Mother Goose—my first book, ever. My mother read it to me as a baby. When I was older, my mother, who would never deface a book, made a point of ripping out a page with racist words. She made a very powerful point that I've never forgotten.

Most Haunting Fairy Tale

The Snow Queen by Hans Christian Anderson

Best Book that I Inexplicably Dislike

Charlotte's Web by E. B. White

Weirdest Childhood Memory Involving a Book

My mother had ordered me to sit at the table until I finished a bowl of her homemade pea soup. Since I hated pea soup, I sat there for hours reading *The Hound of the Baskervilles*, while the soup grew colder and colder, congealing in green, slimy gobbets. I don't remember if I ever actually ate that soup, or if I disposed of it secretly; but to this day, I'm not sure which was more terrifying:

The Hound of the Baskervilles with his great
slavering jaws or my mother's cold congealed
pea soup.

Book That I Wish Was Real
*The Snarkout Boys and the Avocado of
Death* by Daniel Pinkwater (I read this one
as an adult.)

**A List of Books that I Wish I Could Have
Read When I Was a Kid:**
Aaargh! I want to talk about all the books I
love, but there are so many that this list always
spirals out of control in, like, two minutes.

One Book I'd Recommend to Everyone
Stories for Children by Isaac Bashevis Singer

I Can't Believe I Haven't Read . . .
The Harry Potter series by J. K. Rowling

Most Memorable Library, Ever
It was a second-floor room in what seemed to
be a deserted old house in the Adirondacks.
I climbed the stairs to find a dusty jumble

of books lying all over the floor. There was no librarian, no shelves, no checkout, and certainly no due dates. It looked as if no one had been there in years. I picked out several musty old paperbacks to read lying on a cot in our tent back at the campsite. When I was done, I brought them back, and added a few of our books to the pile.

Best Book Binge

In the summer time, our public library allowed us to check out ten books at a time, instead of three. I carried them home, lay down on my bedroom floor, and set to reading them, one after another. By dinnertime, I had finished the entire stack. I staggered to my feet, dazed from so much reading, and felt as if I was returning from a long journey that I'd never be able to describe to anyone.

Favorite Childhood Illustrators

Fritz Eichenberg, Kay Nielsen, Garth Williams, Carl Larsson

Only Dr. Seuss Book I Really Liked
Bartholomew and the Ooblek

Long-Forgotten by the World, but Loved (by Me) Comic Strip
Barnaby by Crockett Johnson

Best Comic Books
Superman
Archie and Veronica

Best Nonfiction Reading
The encyclopedia. It was better than a trip around the world. Flip a page and you didn't know what you were going to find.

Finally, A Few Favorite Books
Hans Christian Anderson's Fairy Tales
The Princess and Curdie and *The Princess and the Goblin* by George MacDonald
East of the Sun and West of the Moon (fairy tales), with illustrations by Kay Nielsen
The Shepherd and the Dragon (a fairy-tale collection; are you sensing a theme here?)
The Twilight of Magic by Hugh Lofting

Pippi Longstocking by Astrid Lindgren (shouldn't Pippiphile be a word?)

The Black Arrow and *A Child's Garden of Verses* by Robert Louis Stevenson

Ellen: *What characteristics do you think a young writer should try to develop?*

Anne: Here is a toolbox of personalities you need as a writer.

1. A kid skipping down the street, happy to be alive
2. A street person muttering to him- or herself
3. A ship's captain setting the course for a voyage
4. A detective sifting through the evidence for the one clue that will suddenly make everything clear
5. A builder raising the walls of a house, brick by brick
6. A monk sitting in silence in a cell
7. A letter writer hoping that his or her message will reach its destination
8. A mother watching a baby grow
9. A spectator at a party

Ellen: *I'm always thrilled when I finish writing a book and realize that it's good. What's your biggest thrill as a writer?*

Anne: For me, finishing a book is usually more relief than thrill. "Made it through another one!" I say to myself, as if lying half dead on the beach after the shipwreck. (And then I hurry to sign on for another sea voyage...) I'm exhausted by the time I complete a book, have no idea if I've written a good one, and often, can't wait for the whole thing to be over already so I can get on to the next one. But I do love being published. There's something about opening a box of books that you've written. There they are: bound, printed, illustrated, and real. But the biggest thrill for me comes from knowing that people are reading my book. One of my first books, *The Salamander Room*, sold out its first printing of 10,000 copies in a matter of weeks. I was so excited by the thought of 10,000 people reading my book that, driving my kids home from a play date, I skidded on ice and drove my car into a ditch. That brought me quickly back down to earth! Since then, my readership has expanded into the millions. It seems to me that whoever reads my books becomes part of me, and I become part of them. That's the real thrill: that so many people carry my thoughts and ideas; just as I carry all the authors I've read and loved.

Acknowledgments

Endless thanks to Megan Shull, who started the magic. Without you, this book would never have been written.

Thanks to all the young writers who e-mailed us over the years with writing questions and who inspired us to write this book.

Thanks to Nancy Mercado, for her acute instincts, sharp editorial eye, and trust in us. It's been a joy to work together.

Thanks to Elaine Markson and Alice Tasman, our wonderful agents, for your strength, wisdom, and belief in us. We can't believe how lucky we are.

Speaking of lucky, we're thrilled that Matt Phelan illustrated this book.

Thanks to Gary Johnson for encouragement, ideas, and humor.

Thanks to Simon Boughton and Roaring Brook Press for bringing Spilling Ink into the world.

We were fortunate to have the amazing Kate Egan as our first reader. Thank you, Kate, for your friendship, insights, and enthusiasm.

Thanks to Toby Freeman, our discerning first young reader.

Thanks to Adam Potter, Fred Schwartz, and Mollie Futterman for enduring hundreds of bad titles, for all-around supportiveness, and especially for honest responses.

Last but not least, thanks to Ian Potter, for patience beyond that of an ordinary four-year-old, and for his ability to entertain himself by diapering the dog.

Authors' Bios

Anne Mazer grew up in a family of writers in upstate New York. Intending to be an artist, she studied at the School of Visual and Performing Arts at Syracuse University. She then went to Paris for three years, where she studied French and French literature and where she began to write.

   She is the author of more than forty books, including the picture books *The Salamander Room*, a Reading Rainbow Feature selection and a 1993 ABC Children's Choice book; *The Yellow Button*; and most recently, *The No-Nothings and Their Baby*. She has also written seven novels, including *Moose Street*, a Booklist Editor's Choice for Best Book of 1992, and *The Oxboy*, an ALA Notable Book and a Notable 1993 Children's Trade Book in the Field of Social Studies. Her short stories have been anthologized in a number of collections, and she has published a collection of her own short stories, *A Sliver of Glass*. She is also the editor of four anthologies: *America Street*, a New York Public Library Best Book for Teens; *Going Where I'm Coming From*, a New York Public Library Best Book for Teens; *Working Days*, a 1998 ALA Best Book for Teens and a New York Public Library Best Book for Teens; and *A Walk in My World*, all of which are widely used in elementary through college classrooms.

Over the last ten years, Anne has been writing the best-selling The Amazing Days of Abby Hayes series, whose main character is a ten-year-old girl who loves to write. There are twenty-two books in the series. She has also written the Sister Magic series for Scholastic.

Her books have been translated into many languages, including Italian, French, Spanish, Hebrew, Polish, Korean, Japanese, and Chinese.

She lives in Ithaca, New York, with her family.

Visit Anne at
www.annemazerbooks.com

Ellen Potter is the author of the award-winning middle-grade Olivia Kidney series (Philomel Books), as well as the middle-grade novel *Pish Posh* (Philomel Books) and *SLOB* (Philomel Books).

Olivia Kidney was awarded *Child* magazine's 2003 Best Children's Book Award and was selected as one of the Books of the Year by *Parenting* magazine. *Slob* was a Junior Library Guild selection. Her newest novel, *The Kneebone Boy*, will be published by Feiwel & Friends in September 2010.

Ellen's books are published all over the world, including England, Finland, Japan, Thailand, Spain, and France.

Raised in New York City, she has made her home in upstate New York.

Visit Ellen at
www.ellenpotter.com